GOOD HOUSEKEEPING
FAMILY LIBRARY

FAMILY COOKERY

GOOD HOUSEKEEPING FAMILY LIBRARY

FAMILY COOKERY

SPHERE BOOKS LIMITED
30-32 Grays Inn Road, London, WC1X 8JL

First published in Great Britain in 1973 by
Ebury Press
First Sphere Books edition 1975

ISBN 0 7221 3948 9

Filmsetting in Britain by
Typesetting Services Ltd, Glasgow.
Printed and bound in Belgium by
Henri Proost & Cie p.v.b.a., Turnhout.

CONTENTS

FOREWORD

Anyone who is genuinely interested in cooking can produce the occasional first-rate meal for a special event such as a dinner party. But the real test of a good cook is to be able to go on producing good meals day after day, all the year round. Cooking for your family calls for special skills, not least because of the range of age groups and individual tastes that have to be taken into account.

So FAMILY COOKERY is a thoroughly practical guide to home catering. Chapter 1, for instance, shows how menus can be dovetailed and adapted so that, in some cases, the same dish can be served to the toddler at lunchtime and the homecoming husband at dinner. A special section, *Meals Without Mother*, offers advice to the inexperienced cook—possibly Father— who has to take over in the kitchen when Mother is ill or unavoidably absent.

FAMILY COOKERY has been compiled and edited by Brenda Holroyd, a former member of Good Housekeeping Institute staff. The recipes she has selected have all been tested in the Institute kitchens and if you have any queries about them, please write to us at Good Housekeeping Institute, Chestergate House, Vauxhall Bridge Road, London SW1 V IHF.

Carol Macartney
Principal
Good Housekeeping Institute

INTRODUCTION

Next to providing a roof, feeding your family well is the most obvious outward sign of your care and concern for their health and happiness. The regular appearance of appetising meals doesn't, of course, of itself add up to a happy family life, but is nevertheless a basic source of content and sense of well-being. So when you stand waiting to be served at the butcher's or lose sleep staying up to ice a birthday cake, you can console yourself that you are doing it from love and affection!

Having said this, it is only fair to admit that the week-in, week-out nature of housekeeping can easily take up a great deal of your time and energy. Some women enjoy buying and preparing food, while others tolerate it only because it is necessary. Your own feeling will depend a great deal on your attitude to cooking; whether you are imaginative in your approach, and whether or not you like experimenting with new ideas and different foods.

But whether you are an enthusiastic cook or would rather be spending the time doing something different, you can make your job a lot easier if you make a habit of putting 'headwork' before 'legwork'. In more ways than one, it pays to think hard before you shop, if you need to save time and money. Getting value for money today requires increasing skills, and with constantly rising food prices few families can afford the luxury of haphazard catering.

So on several counts it is well worthwhile sparing a few minutes every so often to planning the main meals for several days ahead. We think this is so important that FAMILY COOKERY begins straightaway with a chapter containing menu charts for a week, summer and winter. Later in the book, in Chapter 9, you will find some useful tips on shopping and storing.

Isabel Sutherland
General Editor
Good Housekeeping Family Library

Note: In all recipes where a quantity of shortcrust pastry is specified, for example '8 oz shortcrust pastry', the weight given indicates the amount of flour, i.e. 8 oz flour, plus the fat, etc.

Except where otherwise stated, all recipes are for 4 average servings.

1 PLANNING YOUR MENUS

Your family's requirements for the meals that are set before them are really very simple and basic. They want food that they enjoy at the time that suits them; in fact, what they like, when they like. You, on the other hand, as the provider, have to work more or less to a weekly budget, fit into a complicated timetable, cater for individual quirks and preferences, and above all be sure that the food you produce is 'doing them good'.

Eating for health

Producing a balanced diet is an aspect of planning which should become second nature—there is certainly no need to make a fetish of it. All you need to bear in mind, when planning each day's meals, is that you must include some foods from each of the groups containing the necessary nutrients: proteins, fats and oils, carbohydrates, minerals and vitamins (see table in Chapter 9; the subject of nutrition is also dealt with in another title in this series, FAMILY HEALTH).

The following table gives a rough guide to your family's daily dietary requirements, according to these groups.

Milk	Pre-school children: $1\frac{3}{4}$ pints
	Schoolchildren, adolescents: $1\frac{3}{4}$ pints (minimum)
	Adults: 1 pint
	Expectant and nursing mothers: $1\frac{3}{4}$–2 pints
Cheese	1 oz (more, if this is to replace meat or fish)
Eggs	1 each day, if possible; at any rate, 3–5 weekly
Meat, fish	Generous serving; serve liver or kidney once a week
Potatoes	Daily serving, especially for adolescents
Vegetables	Generous daily servings, cooked and raw
Fruit	Raw fruit or tomatoes daily
Fats	Pre-school children: little
	Adolescents, heavy manual workers: about $1\frac{1}{2}$ oz
	Other adults: 1 oz.
	(These figures include all butter, margarine, oils and other fats, in cooking, as spreads, etc.)

Bread	1–2 oz
Sugar	A cheap and easily digested 'energy' food, but lacking in nutrient except for carbohydrate. Take care that sugar does not replace more nutritious foods; excessive amounts lead to obesity, dental decay and other troubles.

These requirements may be fitted conveniently into menu planning in the following way, with variations to suit your own circumstances:

Breakfast	Fruit or fruit juice; cereal or porridge; eggs and bacon, or other cooked dish; toast, butter or margarine and marmalade.
Lunch	Savoury dish or salad; fruit, dessert or cheese.
Tea	Bread and butter, cake, biscuits, in moderation.
Dinner	Meat, poultry or fish; potatoes, vegetables, pudding.

Try to work to a daily meal pattern on these lines, incorporating average requirements to meet the body's needs while allowing for variety—rather than attempting to calculate the necessary nutrients for each meal.

Suiting yourselves

Don't be too rigid when planning what to eat when—the menus and time-tables that work for your friends may not be the ones that work best for your family. Obviously, there will be certain fixed factors that you will have to fit your meals round—such as a child coming home for a midday meal, or the presence of a toddler or baby in the home, but even so, you should have some leeway.

For instance, the Sunday roast is no more than a tradition—why not a salad meal, or a casserole, so you can go out with the rest of the family? And whatever the day, there is no need to stick to a 'meat and two vegetables' pattern for the main meal. Different combinations of meat, vegetable and pasta, or vegetables and cheese not only provide variety but are often more economical.

Similarly, for the second course, a pudding or dessert is more of a convention than a necessity, although admittedly a very popular one. However, since many of the most delicious puddings are also very fattening, if you serve fresh fruit and cheese sometimes it will be better for your family's health.

Using time to save time

The more hectic your day, the more you need to organise your cooking. Quick dishes are not always as time-saving as they appear, and if you stick to them you will limit your choice in any case. You may find it more convenient to prepare a casserole early in the day and then simply put it in the oven before dinner, rather than trying to produce a mixed grill at the same time as getting the children off to bed.

Guidelines for planning

Apart from making sure that each member of the family gets his daily requirements of protein and other essential food elements, there are three points to bear in mind when planning your menus.

Variety and Balance: A substantial first course such as steak and kidney pudding should be followed by a light dessert or fruit, rather than another starchy dish such as Bakewell tart. Avoid sameness of flavour too; strong and mild flavours should complement each other.

Contrasting Textures: At each meal, try to offset a soft texture with a crisp or chewy one. Serve a casserole with a tossed salad and jacket potatoes, rather than spinach and mashed potato.

Colour: Attractive looking food is specially important for children—a chicken fricassee served with parsley-strewn carrots and crisp sauté potatoes looks much more appetising than when dished up with pale leeks and creamed potato.

Linking up with leftovers

Don't plan your meals in watertight compartments—it may seem simpler, but it is not only wasteful but more work in the long run. The key to successful planning for several days at a time is to cook more of some foods than you will need for a particular meal, so that you can link up your meals with 'deliberate leftovers'; e.g., one day's lunch can be devised from the remains of the previous day's dinner. This principle has been adopted in the menu charts that follow.

The weekly joint can reappear in a rechauffé dish next day, in rissoles, savoury pancakes or several other forms. The bone of a leg of lamb or the carcase of a chicken will form the basis of a tasty soup. A bacon joint, after it has been served hot and then cold with salad, can be minced to make fillings for pies or omelettes, or turned into croquettes. Cold Brussels sprouts or French beans make a delicious salad with vinaigrette dressing.

To illustrate the planning principles discussed above, here are two specimen menu plans for a week, one for winter and one for summer. These give suggestions for a main meal and a lighter meal for each day; the lighter meal can be eaten at midday or in the evening, depending on family circumstances.

They are followed by a menu plan for a fortnight, specially devised for a family with a toddler who needs his main meal at lunchtime, whereas his father will need dinner in the evening.

Recipes for the starred dishes on each menu plan are also given in this chapter.

WINTER MENUS

Day	Breakfast	Lighter meal	Main meal
Sunday (The main meal will probably be pre-ferred at midday on Sunday.)	Grapefruit Bacon and egg	Potato and onion soup* Apple pie	Roast leg of lamb with rosemary* Braised carrots Roast potatoes Lemon surprise pudding*
Monday	Cereal Scrambled egg and mushrooms	Cornish pasties Cabbage Baked apples	Lamb and lentil hotchpotch* Tossed salad Queen of puddings
Tuesday	Stewed apples Poached egg on toast	Cod steaks en papillote* Jacket potatoes Green beans Apricot crisp*	Braised beef with herb dumplings* Brussel sprouts Chocolate velvet*
Wednesday	Cereal Bacon and tomato	Spanish omelette Celery sticks Fresh fruit	Cabbage Parcels* Bakewell tart
Thursday	Cereal Sausage and mushrooms	Baked stuffed onions* and tomato sauce Banana fritters	Country pie* Rhubarb meringue*
Friday	Tomato juice Boiled egg	Saucy liver sauté* Carrots Fruit yogurt	Fish chowder* with crusty bread Mixed salad Fresh fruit
Saturday	Orange juice Bacon, liver and tomatoes	Pork and apple bundles* Jacket potatoes Upside down peach pudding*	Cheese and onion pie* Baked whole tomatoes Lemon rice chartreuse*

Potato and onion soup

½ lb onions, skinned and thinly sliced
2 oz butter or margarine
1 lb old potatoes, peeled and roughly
   diced
a chicken stock cube
1 pint water

½ pint milk
½ lb tomatoes, peeled, halved, seeded
   and cut into strips
1 oz cheese, grated
1 tbsp chopped parsley
a few lean bacon rashers

Sauté the onion in butter or margarine for 10 minutes. Add the potatoes to the pan and continue to cook, covered, over a low heat for 10 minutes. Add the stock cube and water, and cook until the potatoes are soft and mushy. Add the milk and either purée the mixture in a blender or stir thoroughly; if using a blender, return the mixture to the pan. Adjust the seasoning and add the tomatoes, cheese and parsley. Reheat before serving. Grill the bacon rashers until just crisp, crumble them roughly and sprinkle over the soup.

Roast leg of lamb with rosemary

4-lb leg of lamb
dried rosemary

slivers of orange rind
water

Wipe the meat and make incisions in the fat with the point of a sharp knife. Insert a little rosemary and sliver of orange rind in each incision. Place the joint in a roasting tin with about ½-in. water. Roast uncovered in the oven at 350°F (mark 4) for 1¾–2 hours, allowing 25–30 minutes per lb. Make gravy from the pan juices. Carve enough meat for immediate consumption, leaving enough for the next day's *Lamb and lentil hotchpotch*. (Discard orange slivers from the remainder.)

Lamb and lentil hotchpotch

2 oz lean bacon, rinded and diced
1 small onion, skinned and chopped
1 clove of garlic, skinned and crushed
6 oz dried lentils
1½ pints chicken stock

16-oz can round tomatoes
salt and pepper
1 lb cold lamb, diced
1 tbsp chopped parsley

Sauté the bacon in a saucepan until the fat begins to run. Add the onion and cook until beginning to brown. Add the garlic, lentils, stock and tomatoes. Bring to the boil, reduce the heat, cover and simmer for 2 hours, until the lentils are soft. Adjust the seasoning, add the lamb and parsley and turn the mixture into a casserole. Cover and cook in the oven at 350°F (mark 4) for 20 minutes.

Cod steaks en papillote

4 frozen cod steaks, unthawed
4 rashers lean streaky bacon, rinded
1 oz butter

1 medium onion, skinned and sliced
2 oz button mushrooms, sliced

Put the cod steaks on separate pieces of buttered foil and season lightly. Fry the bacon until crisp, then drain and chop. Wipe the pan and melt the butter. Fry the onion until soft, but not coloured. Add the mushrooms and cook a few more minutes. Add the bacon. Spoon equal portions of this mixture on top of each piece of fish and fold the foil over loosely. Stand the 'parcels' on a baking sheet and bake at 350°F (mark 4) for about ½ hour.

Braised beef with herb dumplings

10½-oz can condensed vegetable soup
1 lb lean minced beef
2 oz long-grain rice
1 level tbsp chopped parsley
1 egg, beaten

salt and pepper
1 oz butter or margarine
10-oz can whole onions, drained and
    dried

For the dumplings

3 oz unsweetened scone mix
1 oz shredded suet

1 level tbsp chopped parsley

Take 4 level tbsps of soup from can and combine it in a bowl with the mince, uncooked rice, parsley, egg and seasoning. Shape into 16 balls. Melt the butter and sauté the onions until brown and set aside. Add the meat balls to the pan and fry until brown. Return the onion to the pan. Blend the remainder of the soup with 1 can measure of water and pour into the pan. Stir well and bring to the boil. Reduce the heat and simmer, covered, for 15 minutes. Meanwhile, make the dumplings, place them on top and continue to cook, covered, for a further 15 minutes. Serve with Brussels sprouts.

Dumplings

Make up the unsweetened scone mix with the shredded suet, together with the chopped parsley and enough water to mix. Divide into 8 balls on a floured surface.

Baked stuffed onions

4 medium onions, skinned
2 tbsps fresh breadcrumbs
salt and pepper

2 oz cheese, grated
a little milk
a little butter

Cook the onions in boiling salted water for 15–20 minutes and remove them before they are quite soft. Drain and allow to cool, then scoop out the centres, using a pointed knife to cut the top and a small spoon to remove the centres. Chop the centres finely and mix with the crumbs, seasoning and 1 oz cheese, moistening the mixture with milk if necessary. Fill the onions and place them in a greased ovenproof dish. Put small knobs of butter on top and sprinkle with the remaining cheese. Bake in the centre of the oven for 20–30 minutes, until the onions are cooked and browned. Serve with tomato sauce.

Cabbage parcels

1 Savoy cabbage, untrimmed
2 oz butter or margarine
8 oz calf's liver, chopped
1 large onion, skinned and chopped
2 level tbsps tomato paste
½ level tsp grated nutmeg
salt and pepper

1 oz flour
¼ pint milk
3 oz mature Cheddar cheese, grated
a pinch of mustard and cayenne
4 oz cooked long-grain rice
oil for glazing

Carefully remove the unblemished leaves from the cabbage; you need 10 medium-sized leaves. Place them in a large saucepan, cover with cold water and bring to the boil. Reduce the heat and simmer gently for about 10 minutes. Drain and pat dry. Melt 1 oz butter in a pan, add the liver and fry until firm—about 5 minutes. Add the onion and fry until tender. Stir in the tomato paste and seasonings; cool slightly.

Make a thick white sauce, using the remaining butter or margarine and the flour and milk. Add the cheese and season with the salt, pepper, mustard and cayenne. Combine the liver mixture and rice with the cheese sauce. Divide the mixture between the cabbage leaves, fold them up lightly and place in an oven-proof dish. Brush with oil and bake in the centre of the oven at 375°F (mark 5) for about ½ hour.

(See picture on page 17.)

Country pie

2 lb potatoes, peeled
1 oz butter or margarine
3 tbsps milk
1 oz lard
4 oz onion, skinned, peeled and
    chopped
1 lb beef, minced

4 oz lean bacon rashers, minced
1 level tbsp flour
¼ pint beef stock, made from stock
    cube
salt and pepper
½ lb small tomatoes, peeled
5-oz packet frozen peas, thawed

Boil the potatoes, cream them with butter or margarine and milk and season to taste. Heat the lard in a frying-pan, then fry the onion until golden-brown. Add the beef and bacon and cook gently, mixing with a fork, for 5 minutes. Add the flour and mix well, then stir in the stock and bring to the boil. Adjust the seasoning. Reduce the heat and simmer for 5 minutes. Place half the mince mixture in the base of a 2½-pint ovenproof casserole,

15

arrange the tomatoes on top, then add the peas and the remaining mince. Pipe on the creamed potato, using a large star vegetable nozzle. Bake in the centre of the oven at 400°F (mark 6) for about 40 minutes, until the top is golden.

(See picture on page 17.)

Saucy liver sauté

$\frac{1}{4}$ lb streaky bacon, rinded
$\frac{1}{2}$ lb lamb's liver, thickly sliced
1 packet onion sauce mix
$\frac{1}{2}$ pint water

dusting of fines herbes
small packet of frozen peas
gravy browning (optional)

(Serves 3)

Snip the bacon into pieces with kitchen scissors and slice the liver into long strips. Cook the bacon in a dry, shallow flameproof casserole until the fat flows. Add the liver and stir lightly until it turns pale. Sprinkle the sauce mix over and stir in the water, gradually. Bring to the boil, then add the herbs and peas. No additional seasoning is needed. Return to the boil, reduce the heat, cover and cook over the lowest heat for 15–20 minutes, stirring occasionally. Add a few drops of gravy browning, if you like. Serve with buttered carrots.

Fish chowder

1 lb whiting
a bay leaf
a few parsley stalks
salt and pepper
2 oz butter
4 oz celery, finely chopped
4 oz onion, skinned and finely
  chopped

4 oz carrots, peeled and finely
  chopped
1 oz flour
1 lb potatoes, peeled and roughly
  chopped
2 tbsps cream
1 tbsp chopped parsley

Remove the heads and fins from the whiting and clean them; wash under cold running water. Place in a saucepan with the bay leaf, parsley stalks, salt and pepper. Cover with cold water and bring to the boil, put the lid on and simmer gently for 10 minutes. Melt the butter in another pan and add the celery, onion and carrot; sauté without colouring for 10–15 minutes.

Strain the fish, retaining the liquor and making this up to $1\frac{1}{2}$ pints with water. Remove the skin and bones from the whiting and flake the flesh. Add the potatoes and cook, covered for about 20 minutes. Return the fish to the pan. Adjust the seasoning, reheat and just before serving stir in cream and chopped parsley.

Above : Cabbage parcels. Below : Country pie *(see page 15)*

Pork and apple bundles

4 lean pork chops
a little oil or lard
salt and pepper
a little butter

1 orange
2 medium cooking apples
4 sage leaves or dried sage

Remove the rind from the chops. Heat just enough oil or lard to cover the base of the frying-pan. Fry the chops quickly on each side to seal and brown, then season with salt and pepper. Butter pieces of kitchen foil which are large enough to parcel up the chops and place one chop on each piece of foil. Thinly pare the rind from half the orange and cut it into fine strips, then squeeze the juice from the whole orange. Peel and core the apples; cut them in thick slices and arrange over the chops. Top each chop with a sage leaf or a little dried sage and spoon a little orange juice over the apples. Do up the foil loosely around the bundles and place them on a baking sheet. Cook at 375°F (mark 5) for about 1 hour. Serve with jacket potatoes baked alongside the chops. Choose medium-sized potatoes and rub them with butter or margarine before wrapping them in foil. Garnish with orange strips.
(See picture on page 20.)

Cheese and onion pie

2 onions, skinned and chopped
8 oz Lancashire or mature Cheddar
   cheese, grated

1 egg, beaten
salt and pepper
8 oz bought puff pastry

Cook the onions in boiling salted water for 5 minutes, drain well and mix with the cheese. Add nearly all the egg and season to taste. Roll out half the pastry, line a 7–8-in. metal pie-plate with it and pour the cheese filling into the centre. Roll out the remaining pastry to form a lid. Damp the edges of the pastry on the dish and cover with the lid, pressing the edges well together. Flake and scallop the edge and brush with the remaining egg. Bake towards the top of the oven at 400°F (mark 6) for about $\frac{1}{2}$ hour. Serve with baked whole tomatoes.

SWEET DISHES

Chocolate velvet

$1\frac{1}{2}$ oz custard powder
1 pint milk
2 oz cooking chocolate

$1\frac{1}{2}$ oz sugar
a little double cream
a little grated chocolate

Blend the custard powder with about $\frac{1}{4}$ pint milk. Heat the remaining milk with the chocolate until it dissolves. Pour the heated milk on to the blended custard powder, mix well and return to the pan. Add the sugar, bring to the boil and cook for 2–3 minutes. Cool thoroughly, keeping it covered to prevent a skin forming. Fold in the cream and turn into 4 sundae glasses. Decorate with grated chocolate.

Lemon surprise pudding

2 large eggs, separated
6 oz caster sugar
2 oz butter, softened
2 oz flour, plain or self-raising

½ pint milk
3 tbsps lemon juice
rind 1 lemon, grated

Beat the egg yolks with the sugar and softened butter in a large basin. Stir the flour into the egg yolk mixture with the milk, lemon juice and rind. Whisk the egg whites until stiff and fold evenly into the mixture. Turn the mixture into a buttered 2-pint pie-dish. Place in a shallow baking tin containing hot water and bake at 350°F (mark 4) for 40–50 minutes, until golden-brown and lightly set. Serve hot; this deliciously light pudding produces its own sauce as it cooks.

Apricot crisp

15-oz can apricot halves
½ tablet orange jelly
¼ pint boiling water
¼ pint double cream

1 oz butter
1 level tbsp golden syrup
2 oz cornflakes

Pulp or blend the apricots with the juice. Dissolve the jelly in boiling water. Cool it slightly and stir it into the apricot pulp. Divide this mixture between 4 sundae glasses and leave until set. Whip the cream until it just holds its shape and put a layer over the apricot mixture. Heat the butter and golden syrup and stir in the lightly crushed cornflakes. Pile on top of the cream and leave to harden.

Rhubarb meringue

4 individual sponge cakes, sliced
1 lb rhubarb, cut in ½-in. pieces
2 oz sugar

juice and rind of 1 large orange
2 egg whites
4 oz caster sugar

In a 2-pint ovenproof pie-dish put alternate layers of sponge, rhubarb, sugar, with the orange juice and rind. Cover and bake for ½ hour at 375°F (mark 5). Make a meringue with the egg whites and caster sugar and pipe or spoon it on to the baked mixture. Replace in the oven, just below the centre, and bake for a further 10–12 minutes. Serve warm.

Upside-down peach pudding

½ oz caster sugar
15-oz can peach halves
½ oz whole almonds, browned

6½-oz packet sponge mix
1 level tsp cornflour

Butter a 7½-in. ovenproof dish. Sprinkle the sugar to coat the sides of the dish, leaving any surplus in the base. Drain the peaches, keeping the syrup, and cut each in half again vertically. Arrange with the almonds over the base of the dish. Follow the directions for making up the sponge mix and spoon it over the fruit, making sure the sponge seeps between the fruit. Bake at 375°F (mark 5) for about 35–40 minutes, until golden-brown and firm to the touch. Invert it on to a serving plate. Make a peach glaze by blending ¼ pint syrup with the cornflour and bringing it gradually to the boil, stirring the whole time. Pour the glaze over the pudding.

This dish should be put to bake with the *Pork and apple bundles* and jacket potatoes, about ½ hour before these are due to be ready.

(See picture below.)

Pork and apple bundles *(see page 18)* ; Upside-down peach pudding *(see above)*

Lemon rice chartreuse

a 1-pint lemon jelly tablet
15½-oz can creamed rice
2 oz chopped mixed peel

grated rind of ½ a lemon
2 tbsps lemon juice

Pull the jelly tablet apart and place in a graduated measure. Make up to ½ pint with boiling water and stir until the jelly has dissolved. Spoon 2 or 3 tbsps into the base of a 1–1½ pint jelly mould and leave to set.

Cool the remainder of the jelly to a syrupy consistency. Turn the contents of the can of rice into a bowl and stir in the mixed peel, lemon rind, and lemon juice. Fold in the jelly as it begins to set until evenly combined, then turn into the jelly mould. Place in the refrigerator to set; if you want it to set quickly, place it in the ice-cube compartment, but remove it as soon as it is firm. Turn out on to a serving plate.

Jamaican crunch pie *(see page 30)*

SUMMER MENUS

Day	Breakfast	Lighter meal	Main meal
Sunday (The main meal will probably be preferred at midday on Sunday.)	Orange juice Cereal Kippers	Scotch eggs and tomato salad Fresh fruit	Chicken cassata* Green salad Baked potatoes Gooseberry fool*
Monday	Cereal Grilled bacon and tomatoes	Quiche Lorraine* Green salad Icecream and chocolate sauce	Mince and tomato cobbler* Spinach Frothy grape jelly*
Tuesday	Cereal Sausage and fried apple rings	Cheese soufflé Cole slaw Fresh fruit	Baked stuffed marrow* Plum and marshmallow pie*
Wednesday	Fruit juice Scrambled egg on toast	Bacon and rice salad* Cheese and biscuits	Veal fricassee* Rice Grilled tomatoes Strawberries and cream
Thursday	Fresh fruit Poached smoked haddock	Mushroom omelette Green salad Ice cream and fresh fruit	Swiss steak* Broccoli and baked potatoes Stuffed peaches*
Friday	Fruit juice Boiled eggs	Ratatouille (hot or cold)* Fruit whip	Spaghetti Bolognese Green salad Rhuberry*
Saturday	Grapefruit Egg, bacon and mushrooms	All-in-one meat loaf* Mixed salad Jamaican crunch pie*	Summer lamb casserole* Orange sorbet*

Chicken cassata

½ pint chicken stock
1 level tbsp gelatine
¼ tsp Tabasco sauce
2–3 tbsps lemon juice
5 level tbsps lemon mayonnaise
2 level tsps onion, skinned and very
  finely chopped

2–5 sticks celery, chopped
1 small green pepper, diced
1 red-skinned eating apple,
  diced
8–12 oz cooked chicken, diced
1 lettuce

Place the stock in a saucepan, sprinkle the gelatine over the surface and dissolve it over a low heat; do not let the liquid boil. Add the Tabasco sauce and lemon juice and leave to cool. Gradually whisk in the mayonnaise. When the mixture is beginning to set, fold in the onion, celery, pepper, apple and finally the chicken. Turn into a 1-pint ring mould and leave to set. Unmould on to lettuce leaves or other green salad and serve with baked potatoes.

Quiche Lorraine

7 oz bought puff pastry
3–4 oz lean bacon rashers, rinded and
  chopped
3–4 oz Gruyère cheese, thinly sliced

2 eggs, beaten
¼ pint single cream or creamy
  milk
salt and pepper

Roll out the pastry and line a 7-in. plain flan ring or sandwich cake tin, making a double edge. Cover the bacon with boiling water and leave for 2–3 minutes, then drain well and put into the pastry case with the cheese. Mix the eggs and cream, season well and pour into the pastry case. Bake towards the top of the oven at 400°F (mark 6) for about ½ hour until well risen and golden.

Variations
The cheese and bacon given in this recipe may be replaced by 3 oz blue cheese mixed with 6 oz cream cheese. In some quiche recipes, lightly boiled rings of onions or leeks are used instead of, or as well as, the bacon.

Bacon and rice salad

6 oz rice, cooked and drained
¼ pint mayonnaise
4 tomatoes, seeded and chopped
2 sticks celery, chopped
small can sweetcorn, drained

1 small onion, skinned and chopped
8 oz cooked bacon, diced
salt and pepper
2 oranges, peeled and segmented

Toss all the ingredients together lightly. Serve on a bed of lettuce.

Mince and tomato cobbler

1 lb lean minced beef
6 oz onion, peeled and finely chopped
8-oz can whole tomatoes

1 tbsp Worcestershire sauce
salt and freshly ground black pepper

For the topping

2 oz butter or margarine
8 oz self-raising flour
1 level tsp baking powder
½ level tsp salt

2 eggs, beaten
¼ pint milk
2 oz Cheddar cheese, grated
chopped parsley, to garnish

Cook the mince in a thick-based frying-pan until the fat begins to run. Add the onion and cook until tender. Pour off the excess fat. Add the tomatoes and Worcestershire sauce, and allow to bubble until no juices remain. Season well. To make the topping, rub the fat into sifted flour, baking powder and salt and mix into a fairly stiff dough with cold water. Roll out and stamp into 2-in. rounds. Line the sides of a 2½-pint shallow oven-proof dish with the scones, stood on end. Spoon in the meat. Whisk the eggs and milk, add the seasoning and pour over the mince. Top with grated cheese and bake at 400°F (mark 6) for about 40 minutes. Serve sprinkled with chopped parsley and accompanied by spinach.

Baked stuffed marrow

1 medium-sized vegetable marrow
1 packet savoury tomato rice
1 oz butter
1-lb piece lean bacon, minced

¼ lb Bel Paese or Samsoe cheese,
    cut in ¼-in. cubes
1 egg, beaten
salt and pepper

Wash the marrow, cut it in half and scoop out the seeds. Cook the savoury rice as directed on the packet. Heat the butter in a frying-pan, add the bacon and cook, stirring, until sealed all over (about 5–7 minutes). Mix together the cooked rice, bacon, cheese and egg and season to taste. Put the stuffing in the two halves of the marrow and place them together again. Wrap loosely in buttered foil and place in a roasting tin. Bake in the centre of the oven at 350°F (mark 4) for ¾–1 hour depending on the size of the marrow. Remove from the foil and serve at once.

Swiss steak

2 tbsps oil
2 large onions, skinned and
    sliced
1½ lb chuck or blade-bone steak

1 oz flour, seasoned
8 tomatoes, peeled
8-oz can of tomato juice
parsley, for garnish

Heat the oil in a frying-pan and sauté the onions until transparent; if a flameproof casserole is available this can be used throughout the cooking. Trim the steak and cut into 8 portions. Dredge with seasoned flour, and brown in the oil; stir in any excess flour. Add the tomatoes and tomato juice and stir well to loosen the pan drippings. Bring to the boil. Turn into a casserole, cover and cook in the oven at 350°F (mark 4) for 1½–2 hours. Garnish with parsley and serve with broccoli and baked potatoes.

(See picture on page 37.)

Veal fricassee

½ lb back bacon, cut in 2 thick rashers
1–1½ lb stewing veal, cubed
1¾ oz butter
1 tbsp oil
½ a small onion, skinned and chopped

½ pint white stock or water
salt and pepper
¾ oz flour
1–2 tbsps lemon juice

Rind the bacon, trim off any excess fat and cut into pieces about the same size as the veal. Fry the veal and bacon very lightly in 1 oz butter and the oil, but do not allow them to brown. Lift out the meat and place in a 3-pint casserole. Fry the onion in the fat left in the pan until transparent and add to the meat. Pour over the stock and season. Cover and cook in the centre of the oven at 350°F (mark 4) for 1½ hours or until tender. Strain off the liquor and keep the veal and bacon hot in the casserole. Melt the remaining ¾ oz butter, stir in the flour, and cook for 2–3 minutes. Gradually stir in the strained liquor, bring to boiling point and continue to boil for 2–3 minutes stirring all the time. Add the lemon juice and check the seasoning. Pour the sauce over the veal. Serve with rice and grilled tomatoes.

Ratatouille *(see page 26)*

Ratatouille

2 aubergines
3 courgettes
1 small green pepper
½ a cucumber
2 tbsps oil
1 oz butter

4 tomatoes, skinned and sliced
2 onions, skinned and sliced
seasoning
a clove of garlic, skinned and crushed
chopped parsley

Wipe and slice the aubergines and courgettes. Prepare the pepper, removing the seeds and cut in strips. Slice the cucumber. Place the oil and butter in a flameproof casserole. Heat and add the prepared vegetables, seasoning and garlic. Stir thoroughly. Cover lightly and place in the oven at 350°F (mark 4) for 1–1¼ hours, or cook slowly on top of the stove. Serve either hot or cold, with parsley.

(See picture on page 25.)

All-in-one meat loaf

1 lb lean beef
½ lb pork
½ lb stewing veal
½ lb lean streaky bacon, rinded
8-oz can plum tomatoes
1 level tsp salt
½ level tsp garlic salt

2 level tbsps dried celery flakes
1 level tbsp dried onion
8 level tbsps sage and onion stuffing
  mix
freshly ground black pepper
a little powdered bay leaf
2 eggs, beaten

(Serves 8)

Trim the meats and put all three through the mincer, twice, with the bacon. Combine the mixed meats, tomatoes, salts, celery flakes, dried onion and stuffing mix. Add the pepper and a dusting of powdered bay leaf, then blend thoroughly with beaten egg. Turn into a 3½-pint loaf tin lined with kitchen foil. Flap the foil over the top of the loaf and bake in the oven at 350°F (mark 4) for about 1½ hours. Turn out and serve hot with tomato sauce. Delicious cold, too.

Summer lamb casserole

2 lb neck of lamb
1 lb new carrots, scraped and sliced
1 lb small new potatoes, scraped
salt and freshly ground pepper

½-lb packet frozen peas, or fresh
  shelled peas
1 level tbsp tomato paste
fresh mint, chopped

Place the meat in a shallow flameproof casserole. Cover with cold water and bring to the boil. Pour off the water and rinse meat. Replace in the casserole with 1 pint cold water to which 2 level tsps salt and ½ level tsp pepper have been added. Bring to the boil. Add the carrots, cover and cook in the oven at 325°F (mark 3) for about 1½ hours, until meat is tender when tested with a fork. Add the potatoes to the casserole, cover and cook a further 20 minutes. Remove the meat and discard the bones. Cut up the meat roughly and return it to the casserole with the peas and tomato paste. Adjust the seasoning and replace in the oven for a further 10–15 minutes. To serve, sprinkle with chopped mint.

If you make this early in the day, leave out the potatoes and peas. Add them when you remove the casserole from the refrigerator to re-heat it.

SWEET DISHES

Gooseberry fool

1 lb gooseberries, topped and tailed
2 tbsps water
4 oz sugar
¼ pint custard

¼ pint double cream
a few drops of green colouring
a little grated chocolate

For the custard

¼ pint milk
3 level tsps custard powder

3 level tsps sugar

Cook the gooseberries with the water and sugar until the fruit is soft and well reduced. Sieve or purée in a blender. Make the custard as usual and allow it to cool, stirring occasionally. Whip the cream. Fold the custard and then the cream into the gooseberry purée and add a few drops of colouring. Divide between 4 glasses and decorate with grated chocolate. Serve chilled.

For a richer dessert, omit the custard and double the quantity of cream.

Plum and marshmallow pie

8 oz shortcrust pastry
  (8 oz plain flour, etc.)
1 egg, separated
1½ lb plums

4 oz Demerara sugar
4 oz marshmallows, halved
a little icing sugar

When making up the pastry, use the egg yolk to replace some of the liquid.

Arrange the plums with the sugar and halved marshmallows in a 2-pint oval pie-dish. Roll out the pastry on a lightly-floured board so that it is 1-in. larger than the top of the pie-dish. Cut a narrow strip about ¾-in. wide, wet the lip of the pie-dish and press this strip on it. Damp the strip with water. Cover the pie-dish with the pastry lid and press pastry edges together lightly. Trim the edges with a knife, knock them up and crimp them with the finger-tips. Make a slit in the centre of the lid and set in a cool place for at least 10 minutes before cooking.

Plum and marshmallow pie *(see page 27)*

Place the pie-dish on a baking sheet and bake in the centre of the oven at 425°F (mark 7) for 10 minutes. Reduce to 350°F (mark 4) and cook for a further 30–40 minutes. Meanwhile, lightly whisk egg white and beat in enough icing sugar to give a coating consistency. Using a teaspoon, dribble the icing in a web over the pastry. Put under a moderate grill to brown lightly. Serve warm or cold with whipped cream.

(See picture above.)

Frothy grape jelly

1 pint orange jelly tablet
2 egg whites, stiffly beaten

$\frac{3}{4}$ lb grapes, peeled, halved and pipped

Make up the jelly to 1 pint with water. Chill until it reaches the syrupy stage, then fold in the egg whites and the grapes. Turn into serving dishes and leave to set in the refrigerator.

Stuffed peaches

4 large yellow peaches
sponge cake crumbs
a little ground almond
the rind of $\frac{1}{2}$ orange and $\frac{1}{2}$ lemon, grated

juice of 1 orange or a little white wine
juice of 1 lemon
sugar, for dredging

Plunge the peaches first into boiling water and then into cold. Skin them, cut in halves and remove the stones and a little of the flesh. Sandwich the halves in pairs with a mixture of soft peach flesh, crumbled sponge cake, ground almonds, grated orange and lemon rind, and lemon juice to moisten. Place in a shallow dish and spoon over some orange juice or white wine. Dredge heavily with sugar and cook at 350°F (mark 4) for 10–15 minutes until sugar caramellises.

'Rhuberry'

2 lb rhubarb, cut into small pieces
4 tbsps water
1 level tbsp, $\frac{1}{2}$ oz powdered gelatine

2 tbsps water
4 oz caster sugar
$\frac{1}{2}$ lb strawberries

Simmer the rhubarb with the 4 tbsps water until soft. Sieve to give 1 pint purée. Add the gelatine soaked in the 2 tbsps water to the warm rhubarb purée with the caster sugar; stir to dissolve. Press the strawberries through a sieve into the mixture, or use a blender. Stir and pour into a 1$\frac{1}{2}$-pint ring mould. Chill until set, then turn out.

This is particularly good served with a bowl of *Orange cream* in the centre.

Orange Cream

$\frac{1}{4}$ pint double cream
rind of $\frac{1}{2}$ orange, grated

1 tbsp orange juice
1 level tsp caster sugar

Whip the cream until it just holds its shape, add the orange rind, gradually whip in the juice and add the sugar.

Orange sorbet

2 oz caster sugar
$\frac{1}{2}$ pint water
$\frac{1}{4}$ oz gelatine

6$\frac{1}{2}$-fl. oz can concentrated orange juice
1 egg white

(Serves 4–6)

Dissolve the sugar in the water and then bring to the boil. Remove from the heat, sprinkle the gelatine over the surface and stir until this is dissolved. Allow to cool until lukewarm. Stir in the undiluted orange juice. Pour into an ice-tray, and freeze until mushy—about 1 hour. Remove from the tray and fold in the lightly whisked egg white (this should be beginning to form into peaks, but should not be dry). Return the mixture to the ice-tray and freeze until just firm. Serve spooned into chilled glasses.

Jamaican crunch pie

4 oz ginger nuts
2 oz butter, melted
¼ pint double cream
1 small can sweetened condensed
  milk

6 tbsps lemon juice
rind of 1 lemon, grated
8 thick lemon slices
3 oz sugar

Crush the ginger nuts with a rolling pin, or crumble in a blender. Place in a bowl and blend with the melted butter. Use the ginger nut mixture to line a 7½-in. pie-plate, or flan ring, placed on a flat plate. Work the crumbs with the back of a metal spoon to form a shell; the edge should appear just above the plate rim. Lightly whip the cream and fold in the condensed milk, lemon juice and rind, or combine them in a blender. When beginning to thicken, pour into the biscuit shell and chill in the refrigerator overnight. When about to serve, decorate with glazed lemon slices, made as follows: remove the pips and poach the lemon slices in a frying-pan with just enough water to cover them, until tender. Top up the water if necessary to the original level. Remove and drain the slices. Add the sugar to the pan and when it has dissolved, boil to reduce to a glaze. Pour over the slices and cool.

(See picture on page 21.)

MEALS FOR THREE

Day	Midday meal	Tea for toddler	Dinner for adults
1	TODDLER Grilled fish steak, potatoes, peas Fruit and custard MOTHER Grilled fish steak, green salad	Scrambled egg Toast fingers Fresh fruit	Roast beef Roast potatoes, parsnips, Brussels sprouts Trifle (use peaches and put aside some for toddler)
2	TODDLER Cold roast beef with gravy (from last night), potatoes, broccoli Junket and peaches	Chicken soup Sardines on toast Fresh fruit	Chicken soup Shepherd's pie (from remains of beef) Broccoli

Day	Midday meal	Tea for toddler	Dinner for adults
2	MOTHER Omelette and salad	See opposite.)	Baked apple stuffed with walnuts and cherries, topped with syrup
3	TODDLER Grilled chop, tomato, gravy, creamed potato (enough for tonight) Banana MOTHER Welsh rarebit	Egg nest* Milk shake Fresh fruit	Californian chops* Creamed potatoes (gently re-heated) Green beans Cheese and biscuits
4	TODDLER Mince, potatoes, spinach Ice cream, fruit sauce MOTHER Tomato soup, bacon and egg sandwich	Tomato soup Toasted cheese fingers Fresh fruit	Spaghetti Bolognese Tossed green salad Banana creole*
5	TODDLER Tuna, potatoes, peas, carrots Creamy rice and fruit MOTHER Tuna salad	Macaroni cheese (made with egg) Fresh fruit	Beef casserole (make enough for tomorrow) Jacket potatoes Peas Gooseberry rice brulée*
6	TODDLER Meat (from casserole), jacket potato, beans Baked apple, custard MOTHER Egg en cocotte	Cheese omelette Milk Fresh fruit	Beef casserole with dumplings French bean salad Apple crumble and custard
7	TODDLER Poached haddock, tomato, potato, parsley sauce	Cream of chicken soup (add milk) Melba toast Cheese	Haddock roll* (from fish poached earlier) Potatoes, baked

Day	Midday meal	Tea for toddler	Dinner for adults
7	Tropical fruit salad MOTHER Cream of chicken soup, grilled tomato, bacon	Fresh fruit	tomatoes, broccoli Tropical fruit salad
8	TODDLER Braised liver, bacon; potato, broccoli Fruit yogurt MOTHER Toasted cheese sandwich Fruit yogurt	Baked egg Crispbread Fresh fruit	Beef-and-liver loaf* (for tomorrow's lunch, too) Jacket potatoes Apple and celery salad Cheese and biscuits
9	TODDLER Beef-and-liver loaf, potatoes, carrots, parsley sauce Chocolate blancmange MOTHER Beef and liver loaf	Baked beans on toast fingers Fresh fruit	Roast chicken (use packet stuffing) Roast potatoes Sautéed cabbage Chocolate mousse* (adapt midday blancmange)
10	TODDLER Chicken and gravy, rice, cabbage Cornflake crunch* MOTHER Chicken salad and rolls	Cheese soufflé* Crispy bacon roll Fresh fruit	Creamed chicken* (from leftovers) Rice Peas Rhubarb charlotte
11	TODDLER Salmon potato pie, green beans Baked pear, custard MOTHER Vegetable soup, salmon potato pie	Vegetable soup Poached egg Fresh fruit	Veal chop casserole* Jacket potatoes Green beans Baked pears, with fresh orange slices and caramel
12	TODDLER Veal (from casserole), creamed potatoes, buttered leeks Apple pancake	Baked stuffed tomatoes Toast Milk	Baked fish steaks* (bake enough for toddler's lunch tomorrow) Duchesse potatoes (from lunchtime potatoes)

Day	Midday meal	Tea for toddler	Dinner for adults
12	MOTHER Poached egg and cheese on toast		Leek and tomato salad Spiced apple pancakes*
13	TODDLER Creamed fish, potatoes, mixed vegetables Queen of puddings MOTHER Cream of mushroom soup, grilled cheese and bacon toast	Cream of mushroom soup Grilled sausage (grill enough for Mother's lunch tomorrow)	Rabbit casserole* Carrots, parsnips Brussels sprouts Queen of puddings (either heat up over pan of boiling water or serve cold)
14	TODDLER Rabbit casserole (from yesterday) Brussels sprouts Peach jelly MOTHER Sausage and celery salad	Potato and celery au gratin Fresh fruit	Spiced gammon steaks Grilled peach halves Potatoes, buttered leeks Cheese and biscuits

In the following recipes where 3 servings are indicated, one is intended for the toddler at another meal.

SAVOURY DISHES

Haddock roll

4 oz short pastry (4 oz plain flour, etc.)
8–10 oz haddock fillet, ready cooked
1 rasher bacon, chopped

2 oz mushrooms, sliced
freshly ground pepper
a little parsley sauce
a little beaten egg

(Serves 2)

Roll out the pastry on a lightly-floured board to form a rectangle. Skin and flake the haddock. Fry the bacon and sauté the mushrooms in the bacon fat; allow to cool. Mix the fish, bacon and mushrooms with a little parsley sauce (see toddler's menu) and spread over the pastry. Sprinkle with pepper. Roll up tightly, sealing with egg. Place on a baking sheet, brush lightly with egg and bake at 425°F (mark 7) for $\frac{1}{2}$ hour. Serve in slices, accompanied by lemon wedges and garnished with parsley.

Egg nest

1 egg, separated   **1 slice of bread**

(Serves 1)

Beat the egg white stiffly. Toast the bread and arrange the white in a ring on it. Put the yolk into the hole in the middle, and bake in the oven until the egg is set to your taste.

Californian chops

1 oz butter
2 chump chops
½ tsp salt
pepper

paprika
¼ tsp ground ginger
3 tbsps vinegar
2 tbsps marmalade

(Serves 2)

Melt the butter in a frying-pan and brown the chops on both sides. Sprinkle with the seasonings and add the vinegar. Place 1 tbsp of marmalade on each chop. Cover and cook over a low heat for about ¾ hour, until tender.

Beef-and-liver loaf

6 oz lamb's liver
12 oz minced beef
4 oz bacon, rinded
1 level tsp salt
1 level tsp mustard

1 level tbsp tomato paste
1 oz soft white breadcrumbs
toasted breadcrumbs
a little flour
3–4 tbsps red wine

(Serves 3)

Mince together the liver, mince and bacon. Add the salt, mustard, tomato paste and soft breadcrumbs and blend together. Form into a loaf and roll in toasted crumbs. Wrap tightly in foil and bake at 325°F (mark 3) for about 1½ hours. Make a sauce by thickening the dripping with 1 tsp of flour, add 3–4 tbsps red wine and stir until smooth and shiny.

When serving a young child, give him apple sauce instead of wine sauce.

Cheese soufflé

½ oz soft breadcrumbs
1 oz cheese, grated
¼ pint milk, scalded

1 egg, separated
salt and pepper

(Serves 1)

Add the breadcrumbs and cheese to the scalded milk, then the lightly beaten egg yolk, salt and pepper. Beat the egg white until stiff and fold into the cheese mixture. Turn into an individual soufflé dish, set this in a pan of hot water, and bake for about ¾ hour at 350°F (mark 4), until firm when tested with a knife.

Creamed chicken

2 oz butter or margarine
1 small red pepper
4 oz mushrooms, sliced
6 oz cooked chicken, diced
2 level tbsps flour

½ pint chicken stock
4 tbsps cream, or top of the milk
boiled rice
chopped parsley, to garnish

(Serves 2)

Melt 1 oz butter or margarine and sauté the chopped pepper and mushrooms. Add the chicken and leave over a gentle heat. In another pan, melt the remaining 1 oz of fat, blend in the flour and cook for 1–2 minutes. Gradually add the stock, stirring until smooth and thick. Stir in the cream. Pour over the chicken mixture and leave over a low heat for 15 minutes. Serve on a bed of rice, sprinkled with parsley.

Veal chop casserole

1 oz butter
3 veal chops
1 onion, skinned and sliced
2 carrots, diced
4 oz mushrooms, chopped

⅓ pint liquid—½ stock, ½ dry white
  wine
salt and freshly ground pepper
1 bay leaf
3–4 tbsps cream or top of the milk

(Serves 3)

Melt the butter and brown the veal chops. Place them in a casserole. Add the prepared vegetables to the pan and fry lightly; drain and add them to the meat. Pour in the stock and wine, and season with salt and freshly ground pepper. Add the bay leaf, cover and cook at 350°F (mark 4) for about 1 hour. Blend in 3–4 tbsps cream, stirring. Serve sprinkled with chopped parsley.

Baked fish steaks

3 cod or hake steaks
a little oil or melted butter
1½ oz bacon, rinded and chopped

1½ oz cheese, grated
3 lemon slices and parsley or
  watercress, to garnish

(Serves 3)

Brush the steaks with a little oil or melted butter and place in a shallow baking dish. Top with the chopped bacon and grated cheese, and bake at 350°F (mark 4) for 20 minutes. Serve garnished with a twist of lemon and a sprig of parsley or watercress.

Rabbit casserole

3 rabbit joints
1 oz flour
salt and pepper
1 lb potatoes

2 onions, skinned and sliced
chopped parsley
$\frac{1}{2}$–$\frac{3}{4}$ pint stock

(Serves 3)

Coat the joints in seasoned flour. Peel and cut the potatoes into chip-shaped pieces. Place a layer of onions in the base of a casserole and put the rabbit joints on top. Sprinkle freely with parsley, but reserve a little for use as garnish. Top with the remaining onion and potato and add the stock. Cover and bake in the oven at 325°F (mark 3) for 2–2$\frac{1}{2}$ hours. Remove the cover and continue to cook until the potatoes are lightly browned. Serve garnished with the remaining parsley.

SWEET DISHES

Banana creole

3 under-ripe, firm bananas
3 tbsps brown sugar
juice of $\frac{1}{2}$ a lemon

1$\frac{1}{2}$ tbsps water
2 tbsps Jamaica rum
whipped cream

(Serves 2)

Lay the bananas in an ovenproof dish and sprinkle the sugar, lemon juice and water over them. Bake uncovered in the centre of the oven at 350°F (mark 4) for 20 minutes, until brown. Halfway through the cooking time, add the rum. Serve with the whipped cream.

Cornflake crunch

1 tsp butter
1 tsp golden syrup

1 tbsp cornflakes
banana, or other fresh fruit

(Serves 1)

Heat the butter with the golden syrup, add the cornflakes and mix with a wooden spoon until the flakes are evenly coated. Scatter over a favourite fruit.

36

Swiss steak *(see page 24)*

Gooseberry rice brulée

5 tbsps whipped cream
5 tbsps canned creamed rice

10-oz can gooseberries, drained
Demerara sugar

(Serves 2)

Fold the cream into the rice and arrange in layers with the gooseberries in a shallow flameproof dish; finish with a layer of rice. Sprinkle enough sugar to cover the surface. Chill thoroughly. When just about to serve, put under a hot grill to caramellise the sugar.

Chocolate mousse

chocolate blancmange, prepared
    from a 1 pint packet
1 egg white, stiffly beaten

3–4 tbsps double cream, whipped
grated chocolate, or chocolate
    vermicelli, to decorate

(Serves 3)

After making the blancmange, put aside a portion for the toddler. Fold in the egg white and then the whipped cream into the remainder. Chill before serving and decorate with grated chocolate or chocolate vermicelli.

Spiced apple pancakes

2 oz flour
a pinch salt
1 egg
4–5 tbsps milk
a little lard

1½ oz butter
2 oz soft breadcrumbs
4 tbsps apple purée
a little powdered cinnamon
a little nutmeg, freshly grated

(Serves 3)

Mix together the flour and salt. Beat in the egg and sufficient milk to make a smooth batter; this should be of the consistency of single cream. Heat the lard and use the batter to make 3 pancakes. Pile them up between grease-proof paper and cover with a cloth. (Use 1 pancake for the toddler's lunch and keep the others for the evening meal.) To make the spicy apple filling, melt the butter and add the breadcrumbs. Toss with a fork and brown over a gentle heat. Add the apple purée and spices to taste. Divide between the pancakes, roll up and heat through at 325°F (mark 3) for 30–40 minutes. Serve with whipped cream.

2 MAKING THE MOST OF MEAT

If you have been rather conventional in your choice of meat in the past, you will probably find that this item on your shopping list is taking an ever larger share of the housekeeping. The solution is to buy cheaper cuts which will need more preparation and longer cooking, but which pay handsome dividends for your trouble in taste and nutrition.

So don't turn down an unfamiliar but reasonably priced cut because you are not sure how to cook it; your butcher will be able to advise you and, if you pick the right time, he will be happy to discuss the cuts most suitable for particular needs.

Shin of beef, brisket, scrag end of mutton, breast of lamb, bladebone and ribs of pork all make economical and delicious family dishes. Needing less cooking, but equally good, are best end of neck, sliced belly of pork or mince.

How to use the cheaper cuts

Pot roasts and casseroles are just two of the ways of presenting these cheaper cuts. Minced, the same cuts can be used in hot and cold meals; a small amount of minced beef will make hamburgers for two, while more will provide a meat loaf for all the family. If you replace the bone in a shoulder or other joint with a savoury stuffing, or add vegetables to economical cuts during cooking, this not only helps to stretch the meat but also improves the flavour.

When considering *poultry*, don't overlook the possibilities of a boiling fowl. Much cheaper than a roaster, it is perfect for slow casserole cooking.

The cheaper cuts of *bacon*, such as forehock and collar, are just as suitable for many recipes as prime gammon.

Points to watch when buying meat

Beef: The lean meat should be bright red and 'marbled' with small flecks of fat, and the fat a creamy yellow. A line of gristle between the two indicates an old animal.

Lamb: The younger the animal, the paler the flesh; there will be a slight blue tinge to the bones. Imported lamb has firm white fat; English, available only in spring and early summer, has fat of a creamy colour.

Pork: The lean should be pale pink, moist and slightly marbled. There should be a good outer layer of firm white fat, and the bones should be small and pinkish. If the joint is to be roasted, ask the butcher to score the rind deeply and frequently.

Veal: The flesh should be pale pink, fine-textured, soft and moist but not wet and flabby. Bluish or mottled flesh indicates age. Veal bones make excellent stock when boiled and give the special flavour to veal stews and fricassees.

Offal: Ox liver, strongly flavoured and often coarse-textured, should be stewed; calf's liver, very tender and with a delicate flavour, may be lightly grilled or fried; lamb's liver, although more strongly flavoured, is excellent fried or grilled, and can also be casseroled or stewed. Pig's liver has a very pronounced flavour and a soft texture. Casserole it or use for pâté.

Ox Kidney, fairly strongly flavoured, is best stewed, casseroled or curried; calf's kidney, though more tender and delicate in flavour, should be used in the same way. Lambs' kidney can be grilled or fried. Pig's and sheep's kidney, slightly less tender, can be halved and then grilled or fried; or stewed, casseroled or curried.

Heart can be stuffed, roasted or braised. Ox heart needs longer, slower cooking; calf's heart is more tender; lamb's heart, smallest and most tender, has the best flavour.

Tripe is either of the 'blanket' type or 'honeycomb', according to whether it comes from the first or second stomach. It is usually sold 'dressed' i.e., cleaned and parboiled.

Tongue is often sold pickled or salted, in which case the normal cooking time is halved. Ox tongue is usually salted, cooked whole and served cold and sliced. Calf's tongue is also salted; several tongues are often pressed together after cooking and served as above. Lambs' tongues are specially good served hot; allow 4 oz cooked tongue per person.

Poultry: In a fresh (non-frozen) bird, the tip of the breastbone should feel soft and flexible when felt with the thumb and finger. If it is hard, the bird is probably too old for roasting satisfactorily and will have to be steamed or boiled. Look at the feet, too; in a young bird they are smooth with small, not coarse scales, and with short spurs.

Bacon Joints: Should have a pleasant, mild aroma, with the lean part appetisingly pink, fresh and moist—but not wet. Bacon that is too moist doesn't keep well. The fat should be firm and white with no yellow or discoloured patches.

Beef, carrot and mushroom pie

1 lb lean chuck steak
1 oz dripping
¼ lb onions, peeled and sliced
1 oz flour
salt and pepper

½ pint water
10½-oz can small carrots
¼ lb button mushrooms
¾ lb prepared puff pastry

Trim steak and cut into neat pieces. Fry in dripping to seal and lightly brown, then put on one side. Add the onions to the pan, and fry until golden. Stir in the flour seasoned with salt and pepper.

Return the steak to the pan over a low heat and slowly stir in the water. Bring to the boil and check seasoning. Simmer, covered, for 1½ hours. Remove from the heat, add the drained carrots and prepared mushrooms. Turn into a 2-pint pie-dish with a pie-funnel in the centre. Cool it quickly, cover with a pastry lid and glaze with egg. Bake at 450°F (mark 8) for about ½ hour, until pastry is risen and golden-brown.

Savoury mince

1 onion, skinned and quartered
2 carrots, peeled and quartered
2 sticks of celery, scrubbed and
  sliced
8 oz cold, cooked beef

12-oz can of ready-to-serve oxtail
  soup, or ½ pint beef stock
salt and pepper
3–4 level tsps curry powder
1–2 oz seedless raisins or sultanas

Mince together the vegetables and meat, or if preferred, dice the vegetables and mince the meat. Put them into a pan and stir in enough of the soup or stock to give a really moist mixture. Add the seasoning, curry powder and raisins, cover with a lid and simmer gently for 20–30 minutes until the vegetables are soft and the flavours well blended. Stir from time to time, as the mixture tends to stick slightly; add more soup or stock if it becomes too thick. Serve with boiled potatoes, pasta or rice.

Beef upside down

1 medium onion, skinned and chopped
1 oz dripping
1 tbsp chopped parsley, optional
½–¾ lb cold beef, minced

stock or gravy
salt and pepper
3 oz dry breadcrumbs
1–1½ lb mashed potatoes

Fry the onion in the dripping, without browning, until tender. Add the parsley and beef, moisten with a little stock or gravy and season to taste. Well grease a 2-pint round casserole and coat the sides and base with breadcrumbs. Place half the potato in the bottom, spread evenly, add the meat and top with the remaining potato. Bake in the centre of the oven at 375°F (mark 5) for about ¾ hour. Remove from the oven, leave to stand for 5 minutes and then turn it out on to a warm dish. Serve with extra gravy.

LAMB

Stuffed loin of lamb

3–3½ lb piece of loin, boned
3 oz long-grain rice, cooked
a clove of garlic, crushed
2 oz sultanas
4 rashers bacon, rinded, chopped and
    fried

½ level tsp grated lemon
    rind
½ level tsp rosemary
1 egg, beaten
seasoning

Remove the excess fat from the meat and flatten it by beating it lightly. Make the stuffing by blending the rice, garlic, sultanas, bacon, lemon rind, rosemary and egg. Stuff the meat, roll it up and sew together with coarse thread. Dredge lightly with flour and roast, join side down, at 350°F (mark 4), allowing ¾ hour per lb.

Haricot lamb

4 oz haricot beans
2 lb stewing lamb, chopped
1 oz fat
2 onions, skinned and sliced

1 turnip, peeled and sliced
salt and pepper
1 tbsp Worcestershire sauce
parsley or watercress, to garnish

Soak the beans overnight in cold water. Trim away any excess fat from the lamb and brown the meat in hot fat. Add the prepared vegetables and fry for a further 2–3 minutes. Pour on just enough water to cover the meat. Add the drained beans, salt and pepper, cover and simmer on a low heat for 2–2½ hours. Stir in Worcestershire sauce just before serving. Serve sprinkled with chopped parsley or garnished with watercress.

Lamb demi-glace

3 lb middle neck of lamb
1 oz butter
10½-oz can condensed beef consommé
2 strips lemon rind

1 lb firm red tomatoes, peeled and
    quartered
parsley, to garnish

(Serves 6)

Trim the meat free of excess fat. Melt the butter in a frying-pan or flameproof casserole and fry the meat until brown on both sides—about 10 minutes. Pour off the fat. If a frying-pan is used, transfer the meat to a casserole. Add the consommé to the meat with the strips of lemon, cover and cook in the oven at 325°F (mark 3) for 1½ hours. Test with a fork; it should slide in easily.

Arrange the meat on a serving dish and keep it hot. Add the tomatoes to the juices in the pan and reduce by half. Spoon this sauce over the lamb and garnish with plenty of chopped parsley. Serve accompanied by thick slices of courgettes which have been tossed in butter.

Barbecued lamb slices

cold roast lamb
1½ oz butter
3 tsps vinegar
4 tbsps redcurrant jelly

¼ pint stock
a little dry mustard
salt and pepper

Cut the lamb into neat slices. Make a sauce by melting the butter in a frying-pan and adding the vinegar, redcurrant jelly, stock and seasoning. Add the slices of meat, turn them in the sauce until they are well covered and boil gently for 10 minutes. Place on a heated serving dish, pour the remaining hot sauce over the meat and serve at once.

Potato-crusted lamb pie

2 lb potatoes, peeled ·
1 oz butter or margarine
3 tbsps milk
salt and pepper
2 oz dripping

4 oz onions, skinned and chopped
1 lb cooked lamb, minced
½ pint stock
½ level tbsp dried thyme
½ level tbsp chopped parsley

Boil the potatoes in the usual way, drain them, cream with butter and milk, season and keep them warm. Melt the dripping and lightly fry the onions until tender. Add ·the lamb, stock, seasonings and herbs. Bring to the boil and simmer for 15 minutes. Turn into a 4-pint ovenproof dish and spoon the creamed potato over the meat. Fluff up the potato with a fork and place under a moderate grill until evenly browned; or brown in the oven at 400°F (mark 6) for about 40 minutes.

PORK

Stuffed belly of pork

2 lb piece belly of pork
¼ lb cooking apples, peeled, cored
   and cut up

1½ oz sultanas

Wipe the meat and slit it through from one side to make a pocket. Fill this tightly with the apples and sultanas, then sew up the opening with needle and thread. Bake at 350°F (mark 4) for 2½ hours. Before serving remove thread.

Pigaleekie

½ oz butter
1 lb lean pork, minced
1 clove garlic, skinned and crushed
½ lb leeks, cut into large dice and washed
1 small red pepper, seeded and diced

¾ pint stock
seasoning
5 level tbsps long grain rice
gravy browning
parsley, to garnish

Heat the butter in a shallow flameproof casserole, stir in the pork and cook quickly for 5 minutes. Drain off the excess fat. Add the crushed clove of garlic. Stir in the leeks, red pepper and stock. Season well. Cover with a lid and cook in the oven at 325°F (mark 3) for 1 hour. Stir in the rice and simmer on top of the stove for a further 15–20 minutes. Adjust the colouring with gravy browning and sprinkle liberally with parsley just before serving.

Pork hot-pot

4 pork chops
½ lb cooking apples, peeled, cored and thinly sliced
1 onion, skinned and thinly sliced

2 oz fat or oil
3 tomatoes, peeled and sliced
1 lb potatoes, peeled and diced
salt and pepper

Bone and roll the chops and secure them with string. Fry the apples and onions in the fat or oil until golden brown. Put the chops in an ovenproof dish and cover with the apples, onions and tomatoes. Top with the potatoes and brush with melted fat. Season. Add water to come halfway up the meat and vegetables. Cover the dish and cook in the centre of the oven at 350°F (mark 4) for 1½ hours, until the meat is cooked through and tender. Remove the string from the chops before serving.

VEAL

Veal paprika

1 oz butter
1 lb pie veal
6 oz onion, peeled and finely chopped
1 level tsp paprika
1 level tbsp tomato paste

1 pint stock
6 oz long-grain rice
small carton soured cream
salt and freshly milled black pepper
parsley, to garnish

Melt the butter in a frying-pan. When it is about to turn brown, add the veal

44

cut into small pieces; fry briskly. Remove the meat and put it in a casserole. Stir the onion into the pan, fry until tender, then add the paprika and tomato paste. Add the stock, pour the sauce over the veal, cover and cook at 325°F (mark 3) for about 1 hour or until tender. Add the rice, replace the cover and put the casserole back in the oven for a further ½ hour. Gently heat the soured cream in a small pan and fork it through the rice. Season and sprinkle with parsley.

Veal and vegetable pie

2 oz butter
4 oz celery, finely chopped
1 lb pie veal, minced
2 oz fresh white breadcrumbs
salt and pepper
1 egg

1 oz flour
1 lb leeks, finely sliced and washed
½ pint chicken stock, made from stock cube
8 oz shortcrust pastry (8 oz flour, etc.)

Heat 1 oz butter and fry the celery for 5 minutes. Mix together the celery, veal, breadcrumbs, salt, pepper and egg. Form into 16 balls and toss in flour. Heat the remaining butter, add the meat balls, fry gently for 10 minutes and drain. Place the leeks in a 2½-pint oval pie-dish. Put the meat balls on top; add the stock and more seasoning if required. Make up the pastry in the usual way and use to cover pie. Brush with milk and make a slit in the centre. Bake in centre of oven at 400°F (mark 6) for 20 minutes. Reduce heat to 350°F (mark 4) for a further 40 minutes.

Mince and apricot cobbler *(see page 46)*

Mince and apricot cobbler

2 oz margarine
4 oz onion, peeled and chopped
8 oz pie veal, minced
8 oz gammon, rinded and minced
1 level tbsp flour

15½-oz can apricot halves
salt and pepper
9-oz packet frozen sliced green beans
parsley sprigs, to garnish

For the cobbler topping:

8 oz self-raising flour
pinch of salt
2 oz margarine

1 egg, beaten
about 6 tbsps milk

Fry the onion in margarine until golden. Add the meats and cook gently for 10 minutes, stirring, then add flour and mix well. Drain the apricots and cut each half in two. Gradually stir in ¼ pint apricot syrup, bring to the boil and add half the apricots. Season with salt and pepper. Place half the meat mixture in a 2-pint pie-dish. Blanch the beans and put them on top, then cover with the remaining meat and apricot mixture.

To make the Topping: Sift the self-raising flour and salt into a bowl; rub in the margarine until it resembles fine breadcrumbs, then add the egg and mix with enough milk to make a soft, but pliable, dough. Turn on to a floured board and knead lightly. Roll to ½-in. thickness and cut out 12 rounds 2-in. in diameter. Overlap the scones round the edge of the dish; brush with milk. Bake for 15 minutes at 425°F (mark 7). Arrange the remaining apricots in the centre. Bake for a further 10 minutes and serve garnished with sprigs of parsley.

(See picture on page 45.)

LIVER, HEART AND TRIPE
Casserole of liver balls

1 lb lamb's liver, finely chopped
4 oz fresh white breadcrumbs
½ lb onions, peeled and finely chopped
6 oz streaky bacon, rinded and chopped
1 egg, beaten

salt and pepper
2 oz flour
2 oz dripping
14-oz can tomatoes
⅓ pint stock
½ level tsp dried thyme

In a bowl combine together the liver, breadcrumbs, onion, bacon, egg and seasoning. Shape into 12 balls, pressing lightly. Coat with flour. Melt the dripping in a frying-pan or flameproof casserole. Fry the liver balls until evenly browned. If using a frying-pan, transfer contents to an ovenproof casserole. Sprinkle any remaining flour over, add tomatoes and juice, stock and thyme. Adjust the seasoning. Cover and cook at 350°F (mark 4) for 1 hour, turning the liver balls halfway through cooking. Serve with jacket potatoes and shredded cabbage.

Liver en papillote

For each person:

2 slices of lamb's liver
1 oz onion, finely chopped
1 rasher of bacon, rinded and finely
   snipped

2 mushrooms, sliced
salt and pepper
Worcestershire sauce
a portion of frozen peas

Place the liver on a piece of buttered foil; put the onion, bacon and mushrooms on top. Season with salt, pepper and sauce. Add a portion of frozen peas alongside. Wrap up the foil loosely and place on a baking sheet. Cook in the oven at 350°F (mark 4) for about ½ hour. Serve with Brussels sprouts and chipped potatoes.

Stuffed heart casserole

4 small lamb's hearts
4 oz fresh white breadcrumbs
1 medium-sized onion, skinned and
   finely chopped
3 tbsps butter, melted
2 level tsps mixed dried herbs
salt and pepper

2 level tbsps seasoned flour
1 oz fat or oil
1 pint stock
1 onion, skinned and sliced
4 sticks of celery, scrubbed and sliced
$\frac{1}{4}$ lb carrots, peeled and sliced
1 tbsp cider, optional

Wash the hearts, remove any tubes or gristle with kitchen scissors and wash again. Fill with a stuffing made from the breadcrumbs, onion, melted butter, mixed herbs and seasoning. Sew or skewer the opening, coat with seasoned flour and brown quickly in the hot fat or oil. Place in a casserole with the seasoned stock, cover and bake in the centre of the oven at 325°F (mark 4) for 2½ hours, turning them frequently. Add the onion, celery, carrots and cider, if used, for the last ¾ hour of the cooking time.

Tripe Romana

1½ lb dressed tripe
2 tbsps vinegar
2 tbsps oil
2 oz butter
4 oz mushrooms, sliced
1 large onion, skinned and sliced

1 oz flour
14-oz can of tomatoes, puréed
seasoning
4 oz fresh breadcrumbs
1 small packet frozen peas

Cut the tripe into narrow strips about 2-in. long and soak for ½ hour in the mixed vinegar and oil. Melt 1½ oz of the butter and fry the mushrooms and onions for 3–4 minutes. Remove the vegetables, add the flour to the pan and brown slightly. Pour in the tomato purée and season to taste.

    Grease a casserole or ovenproof dish and cover the base with half the tripe. Add the mushrooms and onions and sprinkle on half the breadcrumbs. Place another layer of tripe on this, pour the sauce over, sprinkle the top with the remaining crumbs and dot with the rest of the butter. Bake in the uncovered dish in the centre of the oven at 400°F (mark 6) for 25–30 minutes. Towards the end of the cooking time, cook the peas and use to garnish the tripe.

Liver and peas en cocotte

¾ lb calf's liver, cut into small pieces
1 oz plain flour
3 oz butter
4 medium-sized mushrooms, cut into small pieces

2 level tbsps tomato ketchup
¼ pint beef stock
9-oz packet frozen peas, cooked as directed

Toss the liver in flour. Melt the butter in a frying-pan, add the liver and mushrooms and fry gently, turning, for about 10 minutes. Stir in ketchup and stock, bring to the boil and simmer for 5 minutes. Divide the mixture into 4 heated cocotte dishes and top each with drained peas before serving.

Hot chicken pie *(see opposite)*

Hot chicken pie

4 lb oven-ready chicken
flavouring vegetables
2 oz butter
6 oz onion, skinned and chopped
½ lb sweet red peppers, seeded and
  finely sliced
2 oz green chillis, halved and seeded

4 level tbsps flour
1 pint chicken stock
4 oz mature Cheddar cheese
salt and freshly ground black pepper
13-oz packet frozen puff pastry,
  thawed
beaten egg

(Serves 6–8)

Simmer the chicken in water with flavouring vegetables for about 2 hours. Reduce the liquor to 1 pint by rapid boiling, then strain. Melt butter in a saucepan and sauté the onion, peppers, and chillis for 10 minutes. If preferred, remove the chillis at this stage. Carve the chicken and cut the flesh into smallish pieces, discarding the skin. Place in a 3-pint pie-dish with a funnel.

Stir the flour into the sautéed vegetables and slowly add the strained stock, stirring. Bring to the boil. When the stock thickens, add the cheese, adjust the seasoning and spoon over the chicken. When the filling is cool, cover with a puff pastry lid, scoring the pastry into diamonds with a knife. Glaze with egg, place on a baking sheet and cook in the oven at 450°F (mark 8) for ½ hour. Reduce heat to 325°F (mark 3) and cook for a further ½ hour.

(See picture on page 48.)

Chicken in a pot

1 oz butter
½ lb carrots, pared and sliced
½ lb small or button onions, skinned
¼ lb streaky bacon, rinded and diced
the rind of 1 lemon, finely pared
a good pinch of thyme

1 clove garlic, skinned
4 lb oven-ready chicken
salt and freshly ground pepper
1 lb Jerusalem artichokes
chopped parsley, to garnish

(Serves 6)

Melt 1 oz butter in a flameproof casserole which is a little larger than the bird. Add the carrots, onion and bacon and sauté for 10 minutes. Stir in the lemon rind, thyme and garlic. Remove the vegetables. Place the chicken in the casserole, surround with the vegetables, season lightly, cover and cook in oven at 300°F (mark 2) for about 2 hrs.

About 40 minutes before the end of the cooking time, peel the artichokes, dropping each into a pan of salted water when prepared. Drain them and cut them in pieces and insert among the other vegetables in the casserole. Replace in the oven, without the lid, for a further ½ hour. To dish up, place the chicken on a serving dish and the vegetables round, discarding lemon rind and garlic. Spoon the skimmed juices over and garnish with parsley.

Chicken au gratin

½ pint milk
1½ oz butter
½ small onion, skinned and chopped
1½ oz flour
4 tbsps white wine or lemon juice
a pinch of marjoram
salt and pepper

4 tbsps double cream
8 oz cooked white chicken meat, chopped coarsely
2 eggs, hard-boiled and chopped
2 tbsps cornflake crumbs
2 oz cheese, grated

Heat the milk to boiling point and pour into a jug. Rinse the pan and in it melt the butter; lightly fry the onion, then stir in the flour. Return the milk, stirring, and add the wine or lemon juice, marjoram, and seasoning. Simmer together for 5 minutes. Remove from the heat, stir in the cream, chicken meat and eggs. Turn the mixture into a buttered, shallow, casserole and top with the cornflake crumbs mixed with the cheese. Cook at the top of the oven at 425°F (mark 7) for about 15 minutes, until golden-brown.

Chicken portions

When buying poultry, remember that while a whole bird may be good value for a family, providing a hot meal, a cold meal and soup as well, chicken joints may be more economical when only one or two servings are needed, or cooking time is limited.

Grilled

Brush leg or wing portions with melted butter, then lemon or orange juice. Season with salt and pepper. Pre-heat the grill at medium. Place the chicken, skin side down, in the grill-pan, without the rack. Grill for 10–15 minutes, turn skin side up and grill for a further 10–15 minutes, brushing from time to time with melted butter.

Pan-fried

Cover the chicken portions with seasoned flour, egg and crumbs, crushed potato crisps, or other coating. Put some lard, white vegetable fat, corn oil, or butter with a little oil added to it, into a large deep frying-pan to a depth of ¼–½ in. Heat until a piece of bread just starts to colour. Place the chicken skin side down in the pan and brown, then turn and brown the second side. Cook uncovered over a low heat for 15–20 minutes each side.

Oven-fried

Prepare as for pan-fried chicken. Choose a baking dish that will just take the number of chicken portions to be cooked in a single layer. Use about 3 oz melted butter or margarine for every 4 portions. Place coated side down. Cook at 350°F (mark 4) for 25 minutes, turn, and cook a further 25 minutes.

Coating Variations: A savoury coating for pan-fried or oven-fried chicken can be made by flavouring the flour with curry powder or other spices or with finely grated Parmesan cheese.

Bacon hotch-potch

1 meaty bacon knucklebone
1 bay leaf
6 peppercorns
1 small onion, skinned and sliced

2 pints water
1 lb leeks, sliced
4 oz lentils
pepper

A small hock or end of gammon hock is suitable for this thick, sustaining soup, which is just right for winter.

Soak the bone for at least 4 hours preferably overnight. Put in a large saucepan and cover with cold water; add the bay leaf, peppercorns and onion. Bring to the boil and boil for 20 minutes, then drain and remove the skin. Place the bone in a large casserole, add 2 pints water and the sliced leeks. Cover and cook in the oven at 325°F (mark 3) for 2–2½ hours.

Drain off the stock, straining it into a clean saucepan. Remove the meat flesh, shred finely and place in the stock. Add the lentils previously blanched in boiling water. Bring to the boil and simmer for 1–1½ hours. Season with freshly ground pepper. Serve the soup with crisp French bread or dinner rolls, heated in the oven.

Bacon-capped rice

¾ pint salted water
6 oz American long-grain rice
½ lb firm tomatoes, blanched, peeled and seeded
3 level tbsps chopped parsley
2 tbsps corn oil
1 tbsp malt vinegar

2 oz onion, peeled and finely shopped
1 clove garlic, peeled and crushed
1 level tsp dry mustard
½ level tsp caster sugar
salt and freshly ground pepper
1¼ lb cooked collar bacon
15-oz can crushed pineapple

(Serves 6)

Bring the salted water to the boil, put in the rice, cover with a tightly-fitting lid and simmer for 15–20 minutes to absorb all the water. Set the rice aside to cool. Dice the tomatoes and add them to the parsley. Using a fork, whisk together the oil, vinegar, onion, garlic, mustard, sugar, salt and pepper and blend this mixture into the rice with the tomato and parsley. Finely mince the lean bacon with a little fat. Drain the pineapple, reserve the juice, add the fruit to the bacon and season lightly. Rinse out a large ring tin with pineapple juice and put the bacon into the tin. Cover with the cold rice mixture and press down lightly. Serve unmoulded with a tossed tomato, mushroom and onion salad.

To make individual servings, this can also be moulded in 6 ½-pint pudding basins or breakfast cups.

(See picture on page 52.)

Winter casserole

1 lb collar bacon
1 oz bacon fat or dripping
1 onion, skinned and sliced
2 carrots, peeled and sliced
1 medium-sized swede, peeled and
  sliced

1 medium-sized parsnip, peeled and
  sliced
½ oz flour
½ pint water

Soak the bacon in cold water for 4 hours. Remove the rind and excess fat and cut into 1-in. cubes. Melt the fat, brown the pieces of bacon and then remove from the pan. Add the sliced vegetables, brown gently for 5 minutes. Place in the casserole with the meat on top. Add the flour to the fat remaining in the frying-pan and cook for 2–3 minutes. Gradually stir in the water and bring to the boil. Strain over vegetables and meat, cover and cook at 350°F (mark 4) for 2–2½ hours.

Bacon-capped rice (see page 51)

Pork risotto *(see page 54)*

SAUSAGEMEAT

Bumper sausage roll

3½-oz packet sage and onion stuffing
13-oz packet frozen puff pastry
4 oz lean streaky bacon
1½ lb pork sausagemeat

salt and freshly ground black pepper
1 small egg
poppy seeds, optional

(Serves 6)

Make up the stuffing, following the maker's instructions, and leave until cold. Roll out the pastry to about 15-in. square. Rind the bacon and use scissors to snip it into a small frying-pan; cook slowly until golden. Work the bacon into the sausagemeat and season well with salt and pepper. Form the meat into an oblong shape and place in the centre of the pastry, then pile the stuffing over the meat. Brush the pastry edge with beaten egg, fold the pastry over to overlap and seal and turn it over, tucking the ends under.

Decorate with thinly-rolled pastry trimmings cut in long, narrow strips, brush with beaten egg and sprinkle with poppy seeds. Bake at 425°F (mark 7) for about ¾ hour. When light golden-brown, cover with a double sheet of wetted greaseproof paper. Serve hot, with vegetables, or cold, with a picnic salad.

Pork risotto

1 oz butter
6 oz Italian rice
1 small onion, skinned and chopped
2 level tsps curry powder
$\frac{3}{4}$–1 pint chicken or turkey stock
salt and pepper

a small packet of frozen peas
1 lb large pork sausages
1 cooking apple, peeled, cored and
    diced
2 tomatoes, peeled and seeded

Melt the butter and fry the rice, onion and curry powder until golden, stirring frequently. Add the stock, bring to the boil, adjust seasoning, cover and simmer for 10 minutes. Add the peas and continue cooking until all the stock has been absorbed. If you prefer, the peas can be cooked separately.

Meanwhile, cook the sausages until golden by grilling, frying or baking. Slice into thick rings with a sharp knife and keep hot. Add the apple and diced tomato to the rice, folding it through with a fork. Arrange the sausage (and the peas, if cooked separately) in layers with the rice mixture in a hot dish.

(See picture on page 53.)

Winter sausage casserole

1 oz lard
1 lb meaty pork sausages
1 lb carrots, thinly sliced
4 sticks celery heart, sliced
14-oz can whole tomatoes
$\frac{1}{2}$ pint water

2 level tbsps tomato paste
1 tbsp Worcestershire sauce
salt and freshly ground black pepper
1 lb potatoes, peeled and diced
parsley or celery leaves, to garnish

Melt the lard in a saucepan and brown the sausages. Add the carrots and celery and fry gently, stirring, for about 5 minutes. Add the tomatoes, water, tomato paste, Worcestershire sauce, salt and pepper and bring to the boil. Reduce the heat and simmer for $\frac{1}{2}$ hour. Add the potatoes and continue to simmer until the potato is tender, but not disintegrating. Most of the liquid will have been absorbed during the cooking. Garnish with snipped parsley or celery leaves.

Pork fricassee

1 lb pork sausagemeat
$\frac{1}{4}$ lb streaky bacon, rinded and chopped
$\frac{1}{2}$ pint parsley sauce

8-oz can butter beans, drained
a little cheese

Divide the sausagemeat into 16 balls and fry with the bacon until golden, then drain off the fat. Meanwhile, heat the parsley sauce. Fold the sausagemeat balls into the sauce with the beans. Grate a little cheese over the top and grill until golden-brown.

54

3 FISH

If fish is unpopular with your family, perhaps you need to be a little more enterprising in the way you serve it. A family which is faced with the same kind of fish prepared in the same way week after week can hardly be expected to be enthusiastic. This is a pity because fish is easily digested by young and old, and is rich in food value. A child who has not acquired the taste for fish may refuse to eat it when he is older, so it is a good idea to introduce him to it while he is small.

Tempting a toddler

An individual portion of scalloped fish will often win over a toddler. Remove the bones and skin, flake the fish and arrange it in a scallop shell. Season it, add a squeeze of lemon and cover with a good white sauce. Pipe creamed potato round the edge, garnish with sliced tomato, dab with butter and grill until heated through and nicely browned.

Choosing fresh fish

The flesh should be firm and white, or slightly pink, the gills bright red, eyes clear and scales sparkly. Don't buy fish which has grey, fibrous or watery flesh, or which smells unpleasant. Ideally, it should be bought the day you intend to use it, but in any case it should be stored (in a covered container in the refrigerator) for no longer than a day.

Cheaper varieties

There is as much protein in cheaper fish as in more exotic varieties. Many humble fish can be substituted successfully for more expensive ones.

Coley can be used in the same way as cod or haddock, and makes excellent fish cakes and pies. Its unattractive colour disappears in the cooking.

Rock Salmon (dogfish) is good fried in batter, and served with chips.

Whiting can simply be served with a little melted butter, or can be used for a family pie.

Fresh Herrings can be stuffed with their own roes mixed with cream, mustard and lemon juice; the piquant stuffing offsets the oiliness which some people dislike. Alternatively, dip them in egg, coat them in oatmeal and grill; serve with mustard sauce.

Cured and smoked

Smoked haddock can be simply poached in milk and served with a knob of butter, or used in kedgeree, quiches and other substantial dishes.

Canned

Sardines and salmon can be served in other ways than straight out of the can on to a plate. Tuna and pilchards make tasty pies, fishcakes, risotto and fritters. And many people who don't care for fresh herrings enjoy them in canned form; an economical and nourishing dish.

Frozen

Although frozen fish may appear to be more expensive than fresh fish, there is less waste in the form of skin and bones, and less water content. When buying, check that the packet is frozen hard and follow the manufacturer's instructions as to storage and use.

If using frozen fish in the following recipes, don't overlook it that you should allow slightly less than when using fresh fish. If the fish has to be cut in pieces before cooking, or if it is to be stuffed, remember to allow time for it to thaw sufficiently.

When adapting a recipe to frozen fish, the cooking time may have to be extended slightly; check at the end of the normal cooking time. In the following recipes it is assumed that fresh fish will be used, so if using frozen fish you will need to bear these points in mind.

Fish Provençale *(see opposite)*

Golden glazed cod

4 portions cod fillet (1–1¼ lb)
1 oz butter or margarine
2 oz Cheddar or Cheshire cheese,
   grated

1 tbsp milk
salt and pepper
3 firm tomatoes, skinned and thickly
   sliced

Place the fish in a buttered ovenproof dish, add a few flakes of butter and grill quickly for 2–3 minutes on one side. Meanwhile, cream together the rest of the butter and cheese, work in the milk and season. Turn the fish over and spread the cheese mixture over the uncooked side. Return to the grill, reduce the heat and cook gently for a further 10–12 minutes until the cheese glaze is brown and the fish cooked through. When the fish is half-cooked, add the sliced tomato, arranging it round the dish.

Fish Provençale

1 onion, skinned and chopped
½–1 green pepper, seeded and chopped
2–3 oz streaky bacon, chopped
1 oz butter or margarine
1 lb fillet of cod, haddock or
   whiting, skinned

seasoned flour
15-oz can tomatoes, drained
1 bay leaf
1–2 level tsps sugar
salt and pepper

Fry the onion, pepper and bacon gently in the fat for 5–10 minutes until soft, but not coloured. Wash and dry the fish and cut into 1-in. pieces. Toss the fish in seasoned flour and fry with the vegetables for a further 2–3 minutes. Stir in the tomatoes, bay leaf, sugar and seasoning. Bring to the boil, stirring gently, then cover with a lid and simmer for 10–15 minutes, until the fish and vegetables are cooked. Serve with boiled rice.

(See picture opposite.)

Scalloped cod with cheese

6-oz instant potato
3 oz butter or margarine
1 egg, beaten
1 lb cod fillet
1 bay leaf
2 oz plain flour
¼ pint milk

½ pint fish stock
4 oz mature Cheddar cheese, grated
juice of ½ a lemon
salt and freshly ground pepper
parsley sprigs and lemon slices,
   to garnish

(Serves 4–6)

Make up the potato, following the instructions on the packet. Add 1 oz butter and the egg. Cook over a low heat until the potato becomes firm. Poach the cod in sufficient water to cover, adding a bay leaf. When tender, strain off the fish liquor and set it aside. Remove any bones and skin from the fish. Melt 2 oz butter in a saucepan, stir in the flour and cook for 1 minute. Remove from the heat, add the milk all at once with the fish stock, whisk or beat well and return to the heat; bring to the boil, stirring.

Add the cheese to the sauce with the lemon juice and season. Butter 6 large scallop shells. Spoon the potato into a piping bag fitted with a large vegetable nozzle and pipe round the outside edge of the shells. Divide the fish between them, spoon the sauce over and bake in the oven at 400°F (mark 6) for about $\frac{1}{2}$ hour. Decorate each with a parsley sprig and lemon slice.

(See picture on page 61.)

Haddock and corn au gratin

1 lb fresh haddock fillet
$\frac{1}{2}$ pint fish stock
2 oz spring onions
2 oz Cheddar cheese, grated
2 oz butter or margarine, softened

2 level tbsps flour
6-oz packet frozen sweetcorn
1 tbsp lemon juice
salt and pepper

(Serves 3)

Remove the skin from the haddock. Place the skin in a pan, just cover with water and simmer for 20 minutes to make the stock. Meanwhile, snip the spring onions finely and blend $1\frac{1}{2}$ oz softened butter with the flour. Lightly butter the base of a shallow flameproof casserole and sprinkle in the frozen sweetcorn. Lay the fish over, add 1 tbsp lemon juice, spring onion (reserving a little for garnishing) and seasoning. Strain the fish stock and pour it over, cover and simmer for about 5 minutes until the fish is tender, then remove it. Stir the flour and butter paste into the pan juices, bring to the boil and allow to bubble for $\frac{1}{2}$ minute. Replace the fish and spoon a little of the sauce over it. Sprinkle with cheese and place under a fierce grill, until the cheese bubbles and turns golden. Sprinkle with the remaining snipped spring onion.

Stuffed rolled plaice

2 hard-boiled eggs, shelled and
  chopped
2 oz cheese, grated
1 tbsp chopped parsley

3 oz fresh white breadcrumbs
2 oz butter, melted
salt and pepper
2 plaice, filleted and skinned

Mix the eggs with the cheese, parsley and 2 oz of the breadcrumbs. Bind with the butter and add the seasoning. Spread this mixture over the skinned side of the fillets and roll them up, starting from the tail end; secure them if necessary with a wooden cocktail stick. Place in a buttered shallow ovenproof dish, sprinkle with the remaining breadcrumbs, and bake in the centre of the oven at 350°F (mark 4) for about 20 minutes, until the fish is tender and the breadcrumbs crisp on top. The liquid that comes from the fish during cooking can be strained off and used with milk to make a white or parsley sauce to serve with the fish.

Whiting pie

1 lb whiting, filleted
½ pint milk
1 small onion, skinned
1 bay leaf

a few peppercorns
¼ lb bacon rashers, rinded
creamy mashed potato, (for topping)

For the sauce

Parsley
1 level tsp made mustard

½ level tsp ground nutmeg

(Serves 3–4)

Poach the whiting in the milk together with the onion, bay leaf and peppercorns, for 20 minutes. Meanwhile grill the bacon until crisp, then cut into small pieces. Make up ½ pint parsley sauce with plenty of parsley; use the strained liquor from the fish. Add the mustard and nutmeg. Add the skinned, flaked fish together with the bacon snippets. Turn into a pie-dish and top with potato. Cook until golden at 400°F (mark 6) for about ¾ hour.

Mackerel with mustard butter

3 oz butter
1 medium-sized onion,
    skinned and finely sliced
4 mackerel (10–12 oz each), cleaned
    and with the heads removed

6 oz cucumber, grated
2 level tsps dry mustard
2 tbsps lemon juice
salt and freshly ground black pepper

Melt 1 oz butter in a large frying-pan. Add the onion and cook until soft, but not coloured. Drain and remove the onion. Add another 1 oz butter to the pan and lay the mackerel in it side by side. Fry gently for 20 minutes, turning them over halfway through the cooking time. Remove the mackerel and keep them warm. Wipe the pan clean with absorbent kitchen paper. Melt the remaining 1 oz butter in the pan, stir in the cucumber, cooked onion, mustard blended with lemon juice and seasoning and heat through. Return the mackerel to the pan, spoon the mustard-butter over the fish and serve immediately.

Gooseberry stuffed mackerel

4 mackerel, cleaned
a little butter
10-oz can gooseberries,
drained

4 small tomatoes, sliced
freshly ground pepper
$\frac{1}{2}$ level tsp nutmeg

Place each mackerel on a piece of well-buttered foil and stuff with the gooseberries. Lay the tomato slices on top of the fish and sprinkle with pepper and nutmeg. Parcel up and place on a baking sheet. Bake at 325°F (mark 3) for $\frac{1}{2}$ hour.

Herring fillets Normandy style

4 herrings (about 1 lb), cleaned
seasoned flour
2 oz butter or margarine
2 tbsps oil

2 eating apples
juice of $\frac{1}{2}$ a lemon
freshly ground pepper
chopped parsley

Cut each herring in half down the centre and dip in seasoned flour. Fry in 1 oz butter and the oil, until crisp and golden on both sides. Arrange the fish, overlapping, on a serving dish and keep them warm. Peel and core the apples and cut in eighths. Add 1 oz butter to the pan and sauté the apple segments until they are tender, but still whole. Add the lemon juice and pepper and if needed, a little more butter. Spoon over the herrings and serve hot, with a good sprinkling of chopped parsley.

SMOKED AND CANNED

Cheesy fish balls

1 lb smoked haddock
2 oz butter or margarine
2 oz plain flour
$\frac{1}{2}$ pint milk
4 oz Cheddar cheese, grated

salt, pepper and made mustard
beaten egg
fresh white breadcrumbs
6 tbsps corn oil

Poach the haddock in sufficient water to cover it. When tender, drain, remove the flesh and flake it, discarding the bones. Melt the butter, stir in the flour and cook without colouring for about 3 minutes. Gradually add the milk, a little at a time, beating between each addition. Cook gently for 5 minutes. Beat in the cheese, fold in the flaked fish and season to taste with salt, pepper and mustard. Spread on a flat plate to cool.

Shape the mixture into 12 balls, coat them in flour and dip them in beaten egg and breadcrumbs. Heat the oil in a frying-pan and fry the fish balls quickly until golden-brown, turning them frequently. Serve at once with tomato chutney.

Above : Scalloped cod *(see page 57)*. Below : Sardine quiche *(see page 63)*

Kedgeree

6 oz long-grain rice
1 tbsp onion, skinned and chopped
3 oz butter or margarine
6 oz cooked smoked haddock,
   skinned and boned

2 eggs, hard-boiled and chopped
seasoning
chopped parsley
1 tbsp cream (optional)

Boil the rice and drain thoroughly. Cook the onion in the butter, but do not let it brown. Stir in the flaked fish and hard-boiled egg and heat through. Season well, add the hot rice, and stir lightly. Turn on to a hot dish and sprinkle well with chopped parsley. A little cream may be folded through the kedgeree just before serving.

Smoked haddock and cheese flan

8-in. baked shortcrust flan case
$\frac{1}{2}$ lb smoked haddock
$\frac{1}{4}$ pint of water
the juice of 1 small lemon
1 oz butter or margarine
1 small onion, skinned and chopped

2 oz mushrooms, diced
2 eggs
3 tbsps fresh single cream
4 oz plain cottage cheese
salt and pepper
chopped parsley

(Serves 4–6)

Prepare and bake the flan case. Poach the haddock in a pan with the water and half the lemon juice. Drain the fish, discard any bones or skin and flake the flesh. Melt the butter in a pan and cook the onion for a few minutes. Add the mushrooms and cook a further few minutes. Combine the fish and vegetables; spread over flan base. Beat the eggs, add the cream, cheese and remaining lemon juice. Adjust the seasoning and pour over the fish mixture. Bake in the oven at 350°F (mark 4) for about $\frac{1}{2}$ hour until set and golden. Serve hot or cold, garnished with parsley.

Flaked tuna roll

1 egg
5 fl. oz soured cream
7-oz can tuna steak
$1\frac{1}{2}$ oz fresh white breadcrumbs

salt and pepper
$\frac{1}{2}$ lb ready made puff pastry
2 eggs, hard-boiled and sliced
beaten egg to glaze

Beat the egg with the cream and stir into the drained, flaked tuna with the breadcrumbs. Season well with salt and pepper. Roll out the pastry into an oblong 10 in. by 14 in. From one side cut 8 strips, 10 in. long and $\frac{1}{4}$ in. wide for decoration and set aside. Spoon half the fish down the centre of the pastry. Cover with a layer of hard-boiled egg slices and top with the remaining fish mixture. Brush the edges with beaten egg, flap over the pastry sides, overlap them and seal. Place join side down on baking sheet. Brush with beaten egg and decorate with a lattice of pastry strips. Bake at 425°F (mark 7) for about $\frac{1}{2}$ hour until golden-brown.

(See picture on page 64.)

Sardine quiche

4 oz shortcrust pastry (4 oz flour, etc.)
$\frac{1}{2}$ lb onions, skinned
1 oz butter or margarine
salt and freshly ground black pepper

$4\frac{1}{2}$-oz can sardines in olive oil
2 large eggs
milk
lemon wedges

Line an $8\frac{1}{2}$-in. loose-bottomed fluted flan tin with the thinly rolled pastry. Place on a baking sheet. Thinly slice the onions and cook in the melted butter until soft, but not brown. Season and cool. Drain the sardines and discard the tails. Place the onions in the flan base, piled up a little under the sardines, which should be placed like the spokes of a wheel. Beat the eggs, season, and make up to $\frac{1}{2}$ pint with the milk. Carefully spoon the egg custard mixture round the sardines. Bake in the oven at 400°F (mark 6) for 20 minutes. Reduce the heat to 325°F (mark 3) and cook for a further 20 minutes. Serve hot or cold, with lemon wedges.

(See picture on page 61.)

Salmon and cheese flan

6 oz shortcrust pastry
(6 oz flour, etc.)
1 large egg, beaten
$\frac{1}{4}$ pint milk
2 oz onion, skinned and grated

salt and pepper
$7\frac{1}{2}$-oz can pink salmon
$3\frac{1}{2}$ oz cheese, grated
cucumber for garnish

(Serves 4–6)

Roll out the pastry and use to line an $8\frac{1}{2}$-in. loose-bottomed fluted flan tin. Place on a baking sheet. Whisk together the egg, milk and onion. Season lightly with salt and pepper. Drain the salmon and discard any dark skin and bone. Flake the fish and spoon it into the bottom of the pastry case. Scatter the cheese evenly over the fish and spoon the egg custard mixture over. Bake in the centre of the oven at 400°F (mark 6) for 15 minutes. Reduce to 350°F (mark 4) for about a further 25 minutes until golden-brown and set.

Remove the flan ring and leave to cool. Garnish with wafer-thin slices of cucumber, dressed with French dressing, drained and then twisted to give height.

(See picture on page 64.)

Tuna-filled tomatoes

4 large tomatoes
2 oz butter or margarine
1 onion, skinned and chopped
4 oz button mushrooms, sliced

7-oz can tuna steak, drained
2 tbsps chopped parsley
lemon wedges, to garnish

Remove the top from each tomato, cutting in a zig-zag fashion. Carefully scoop out the soft core and pips and discard these. Place the tomatoes on a baking sheet. Heat the butter in frying-pan, add the onion and cook until soft, without colouring. Add the mushrooms and continue cooking for a few minutes. Flake the fish and add it to the pan, together with the parsley. Mix well together. Divide the mixture between the tomatoes. Cover with foil and bake in the centre of the oven at 350°F (mark 4) for about 20 minutes to $\frac{1}{2}$ hour. Serve garnished with lemon wedges or slices.

(See picture below, right.)

Left: Salmon and cheese flan; Flaked tuna roll *(see pages 63 and 62)*. Right: Tuna-filled tomatoes *(see above)*

4 VEGETABLES

Vegetables are all too obviously incorporated in most meals as an afterthought. Yet if you confine them to their traditional role in English cookery as an accompaniment to complement fish or meat, you will deprive yourself of the great variety of other ways in which they can be used.

Many vegetables, such as asparagus, corn on the cob and globe artichokes, are best served as a dish on their own. There are others that can very well, in combination with meat and cheese, form the main course. Stuffed cabbage, marrow or peppers, leek and cheese pie and moussaka are a few of the many sustaining and delicious possibilities. The tomato (strictly speaking, a fruit, but normally regarded as a vegetable) is an ingredient in innumerable savoury dishes suitable for lunch or supper.

Golden rules

However, whether you use vegetables as a main dish, a separate dish or as an accompaniment, the rules for vegetable cookery are the same. Buy them as fresh as possible, use them as soon as you can, and if boiling, don't drown them or overcook them. Drain them well, chopping green vegetables in a colander to remove the water. Remember that the right seasoning or garnish may make all the difference between an insipid, unattractive bowlful and one that equally pleases taste and eye.

Baking: As an alternative to boiling, steaming, pressure cooking and frying, try baking vegetables with the joint. Or cook them in a fireproof dish with some hot dripping. Marrow, parsnips. Jerusalem artichokes, and carrots are good done in this way. Cook at 400°F (mark 6) for $\frac{3}{4}$–1 hour.

Braising: Onions, leeks, celery and many root vegetables are delicious braised in a covered casserole. Fry them until lightly browned, season, add a little stock, and cover the dish. Cook gently until tender, then drain off the liquor and reduce it by boiling until it is of a glazing consistency. Pour the glaze over the vegetables and garnish with a little parsley.

Frying: When frying vegetables, don't cover them with a lid or they will soon go limp and soggy. They should be served piping hot.

Dressing Them Up: The individual taste of a vegetable can often be brought out by using a proprietary blend of seasoned salt and pepper.

Chopped herbs or powdered spice give added flavour. Chives or dill improve mashed potato, tarragon is good with courgettes, while a pinch of nutmeg gives a lift to cabbage or spinach. A good topping for carrots, green beans, broccoli and cauliflower can be made as follows: lightly fry half a breakfast cupful of dry white breadcrumbs in 2 oz of butter, gently stirring all the time, until golden brown. Leeks, marrow, cauliflower and broad beans are often improved by a savoury white sauce.

Make the most of them
There is usually some point in the year when even a luxury vegetable comes down in price for a short time, so we have included recipes for asparagus, avocados and globe artichokes. Many people do not take advantage of the very wide range of imported vegetables, perhaps because they are not quite sure how to cook them. For this reason recipes have been given for yams, aubergines and courgettes.

However, if you have a child with a baked bean fixation, you may have to beguile him gradually into being more adventurous. A good trick is to mix a vegetable that he hasn't had before with one that he knows and likes. Start on an unambitious level, perhaps by mashing swedes or turnips with carrots, or throwing in a few mushrooms when frying tomatoes, before trying to introduce him to more exotic delights.

Artichokes (Globe)

The fact that these are tackled with the fingers gives them a special appeal so far as many children are concerned. Cooking is easy, but they must be soaked in cold water for about half an hour beforehand to ensure that they are thoroughly cleaned. Drain well before cooking them in gently boiling water for 20–40 minutes, depending on size, until leaves can be pulled out easily. Serve with melted butter or Hollandaise sauce.

When eating a globe artichoke, pull off the leaves one after another with the fingers, dip the soft end of each leaf in butter or sauce and suck it. When you reach the centre use a knife and fork to remove the choke (or soft flowery part), which is the chief delicacy, from the surrounding hairy part, which is inedible.

Artichokes (Jerusalem)

After scrubbing them, peel quickly and keep under cold water to prevent discoloration. (A squeeze of lemon juice or a few drops of vinegar helps to keep them a good colour.) Cook until just soft in boiling salted water to which a little lemon juice or vinegar has been added. This will take about ½ hour. Drain, and garnish with finely chopped parsley. Alternatively, serve with a white, cheese, or Hollandaise sauce, or with melted butter. They can also be peeled, sliced and fried.

Asparagus

Allow 1½ lb for 4 people. When fresh, the spears are firm and stiff. To prepare, remove the woody end of the stalks and scrape the white part lightly, removing any coarse spines. Tie in small bundles. To cook, place the bundles upright in a pan of boiling salted water for 10 minutes then lay them flat and simmer for a further 10 minutes or so. Drain thoroughly and untie. If you use an asparagus cooker, leave them upright throughout, cooking the tender heads in the steam.

Serve with melted butter or Hollandaise sauce; or serve cold with vinaigrette dressing or mayonnaise.

Aubergines

These can be served in various ways. Sautéed, fried (first egg-and-crumb the slices or dip them in batter) stuffed (when halved) or baked (in slices, sprinkled with breadcrumbs and dotted with butter). Serve baked aubergines with tomato sauce. If you sprinkle the aubergines with salt and leave them for ½ hour or so, then drain them before they are cooked, this helps to draw off some of the water content.

Aubergines are an essential part of Greek *Moussaka* (see page 85), and are among the vegetables used in *Ratatouille* (page 25), which is delicious served hot as a main course or cold as a starter; it is also good as an omelette filling, as an accompaniment for fish, or, to eke it out at times of the year when the ingredients are expensive, with rice.

Aubergines southern-style

4 aubergines (about 1½ lb)
salt
flour, optional
4–5 tbsps cooking oil
2 oz butter

small clove of garlic, skinned and
  crushed
2 tbsps chopped parsley (optional)
freshly milled black pepper

Wipe the aubergines with a damp cloth; discard the stem and calyx. Cut into ½-in. slices and arrange in a wide dish before sprinkling with salt. Leave for ½–1 hour. Drain thoroughly, wipe well and dip, if wished, in flour. Heat half the oil and butter; when hot, fry the aubergine slices, a few at a time, until brown and tender. Drain and keep hot in a serving dish. Add the remaining oil and butter to the pan as required. When all the sliced aubergine is cooked, pour off all but 1 tbsp of the pan drippings; add the crushed garlic and the parsley, if used. Spoon the sauce over the aubergine, then add freshly milled pepper. Serve as an accompaniment.

(See picture on page 68.)

Aubergines southern-style *(see page 67)*

Aubergines with savoury stuffing

2 medium-sized aubergines
2 oz lean ham, diced
1 tbsp chopped parsley
1 tomato, skinned and chopped
2 oz fresh breadcrumbs

$\frac{1}{2}$ an onion, skinned and grated
salt and pepper
4 oz Cheddar cheese, grated
a little stock or beaten egg to bind,
  if necessary

Wipe the aubergines and remove the stalks. Cut in half lengthwise and scoop out the seed area from the centre of each, leaving a $\frac{1}{4}$-in. thick 'shell'. Make the stuffing by combining the ham, parsley, tomato, crumbs, onion, seasoning, and 2 oz of the cheese with the roughly chopped aubergine flesh. Moisten with a little stock or beaten egg, and fill the aubergine shells. Sprinkle with the remaining grated cheese, cover with a lid or foil and bake in the centre of the oven at 400°F (mark 6) for 15–20 minutes until cooked. Uncover and cook for a further 5–10 minutes until crisp and brown on top. Serve hot, with a tomato sauce.

Avocados

Strictly speaking, this is a fruit rather tnan a vegetable, but is usually given a savoury dressing, and served as an hors d'oeuvre or 'starter'. You can tell if an avocado is ripe if the flesh gives slightly to gentle pressure when held in the hand; it should have the soft consistency of butter. Either buy avocados ready for use the same day, or let them ripen at home for several days. Although the avocado can be served in dozens of ways, with different fillings and dressings, it is delicious when served simply as follows (allow half to each person):

Slice carefully lengthwise, using a stainless steel knife and working round the large stone. Separate into halves by gently rotating in opposite directions. Lift the pointed end of the stone with the tip of the knife and take it out, then brush the exposed surfaces with lemon juice. Serve with the cavity filled with a well-seasoned oil and vinegar dressing made by blending together $\frac{1}{4}$ level tsp each of salt, dry mustard and sugar, and $\frac{1}{8}$ level tsp pepper, with 1 tbsp wine vinegar. Beat in 2 tbsps oil gradually. (See also the salad section at the end of this chapter.)

Beans

Runner and French Beans are good served with carrots. Put $\frac{1}{2}$ lb of young carrots, scraped and thinly sliced, in 1 in. water, with salt and pepper, in a thick saucepan and cook for 10 minutes, with the lid on. Add 1 lb runner beans, stringed and thinly sliced, and 2 tbsps cooking oil, and continue cooking for a further 20 minutes, or until soft. If French beans are used, they may be cooked whole.

Broad Beans are at their most delicious when they are only a few ins. long and can be cooked and eaten in their pods. Whether you serve them this way, or shelled, cook them in just a little boiling salted water for about 20 minutes. Be lavish with the melted butter if you are serving them in their pods. Serve shelled broad beans with a thin white sauce to which you have added a little cream, plenty of parsley, a dash of lemon juice and a pinch of nutmeg. Top with crisp crumbled streaky bacon rashers.

Beetroots

These have to be handled carefully during preparation; cut off the stalks about 1 in. above the root and wash the beets, taking care not to damage the skin, or they will bleed during cooking. They should be cooked in salted water until tender; small new beetroots take about 40–45 minutes, others longer, the average time being about 2 hours. Drain, remove the skins, and serve hot, coated with a savoury white sauce, or leave them to cool and serve them sliced, with or without a little vinegar.

Beetroot diable

2 lb small beetroot
4 oz onion, skinned
4 tbsps vinegar
10 peppercorns
1 level tbsp tomato paste
1 oz dark brown sugar
pinch of cayenne pepper

$\frac{1}{2}$ level tsp dry mustard
1 tbsp Worcestershire sauce
$\frac{3}{4}$ pint beef stock made with a stock cube
2 level tbsps cornflour
2 tbsps cold water

(Serves 6)

Cook the beetroot in boiling salted water until tender—about 2 hours. Drain, peel, and keep warm. Chop the onion finely and add to the vinegar and peppercorns in a saucepan. Reduce over medium heat until only 1 tbsp of liquid remains. Stir in the tomato paste, sugar, cayenne, mustard and Worcestershire sauce. Pour the stock over and bring to the boil. Blend the cornflour with cold water; pour the bubbling liquid over and heat for a few minutes. Arrange the beetroot in a serving dish and pour the sauce over.
(See picture on page 72.)

Glazed beetroots

12 small beetroots, cooked
1 oz butter
1 level tsp sugar
salt and pepper
grated rind of 1 lemon

1 tsp chopped chives
2 tsps chopped parsley
juice of $\frac{1}{2}$ lemon
1 tbsp capers

Remove the skin, stalk and root end from the beetroots. Melt the butter in a saucepan and add the beetroots, sugar, salt, pepper and lemon rind. Toss the beetroots in the pan over a medium heat until they are well coated; add the remaining ingredients, heat through and serve, at once.

Broccoli

Cook white broccoli as you would cauliflower; the purple and green varieties, which have a more delicate flavour, can be served plain, buttered or with Hollandaise sauce. Or try them this way: gently fry some scissor-snipped chives and grated onion in a little butter, add a few drops of lemon juice and a little crushed garlic and pour over the cooked broccoli. Top with toasted shredded almonds.

Brussels sprouts

Children often find these unpalatable. Try cooking them with frozen cut green or runner beans—$\frac{1}{2}$ lb to each 1 lb of sprouts—or celery sticks—3–4 sticks to

1 lb of sprouts. Or cook them as usual, drain well, and put into a shallow flameproof dish; cover with a thick cheese sauce, sprinkle with breadcrumbs and grated cheese mixed together, and brown in the oven or under the grill.

Cabbage

Frequently underrated, even more frequently over-cooked, cabbage deserves better treatment than it usually receives. You can help to reduce the cooking odours if you put ½ lemon in the pan or steamer in which the cabbage is being cooked. After removing the coarse outer leaves, halve the cabbage and remove the hard centre stalk. Shred finely and cook rapidly in about 1 in. of boiling salted water for about 10–15 minutes, or until cooked. Drain well.

The final stages can make all the difference to this vegetable. Toss it with a knob of butter, a sprinkling of pepper and a pinch of grated nutmeg (optional). Or try it with soured cream. Drain and chop up some lightly cooked cabbage, put it in a shallow fireproof dish, sprinkle with a little paprika pepper and spread the contents of a small carton of soured cream over the top. Brown lightly in a fairly hot oven for about 15 minutes.

Stuffed cabbage

1 oz lard
½ lb onions, skinned and chopped
4 oz long-grain rice (uncooked)
½ lb pork, minced
½ lb veal, minced
6½-oz can of pimentos, drained and chopped

½ level tsp chilli powder
dash of Tabasco
2 tbsps mango chutney
¼ pint chicken stock, made with a stock cube
a 3 lb tight-leaved cabbage

Heat the lard in a frying-pan, add the onions and fry gently until light golden-brown. Add the rice and fry gently for a few minutes, stirring. Add the minced meats and fry until browned, stirring. Add the pimentos, chilli powder, Tabasco, chutney and stock. Bring to the boil, cover and simmer gently for 20 minutes. Meanwhile, remove the centre leaves of the trimmed cabbage to form a cavity and then stuff with the meat mixture. Wrap in foil and cook in a pan of boiling water for ½ hour.

(See picture on page 73.)

Carrots

Children will often eat raw carrots—either cut into sticks or grated and sprinkled over other vegetables—in preference to having them cooked. But try tempting them with baby carrots, cooked like this. Scrape the carrots, cut off the tops and put into a small, deep saucepan with a knob of butter, 2–3 level tsps sugar, a little black pepper, and just enough chicken stock to cover. Cook gently for 20–25 minutes. By this time the stock should have been absorbed and the carrots should be glistening and tender. Serve dressed with chopped parsley.

Alternatively, if you add 1½ tbsp chopped fresh mint to the water in which young carrots are cooked, it makes a remarkable difference; garnish the carrots with mint sprigs when serving. These are delicious with roast lamb.

Carrots with bacon

Rind some small strips of streaky bacon and fry. Remove them from the pan and put in some sliced carrots and a little diced onion; cover with a little water and cook gently until most of the water has evaporated and the vegetables are tender. Drain, and return the bacon strips to heat through before serving.

Golden carrots

1½ lb carrots, scraped and thinly
    sliced
½ lb onions, skinned and thinly
    sliced
2 oz fat
½ oz flour
stock
salt and pepper
1 tbsp chopped parsley
1 egg yolk

Fry the carrots and onions lightly in the fat, add the flour and just enough stock to cover, then season with salt and pepper to taste. Simmer gently for about ½ hour, stir in the parsley and egg yolk and serve at once.

Left: Beetroot diable *(see page 70)*. Right: Cauliflower Niçoise *(see opposite)*

Cauliflower Niçoise

1 medium-sized cauliflower	1 oz butter
salt	1 small clove of garlic
1 small onion	freshly ground black pepper
½ lb firm tomatoes	1 tbsp chopped parsley

Divide the cauliflower head into florets and cook in boiling salted water for about 10 minutes; drain thoroughly. Meanwhile have ready the Niçoise mixture. Skin the onion and slice the flesh finely; skin the tomatoes, halve, discard the pips, and cut the flesh into squares. Melt the butter and fry the onion until soft. Lightly stir in the tomato and skinned and crushed garlic. Heat through; season with black pepper. Arrange the cauliflower in a serving dish, top with the tomato mixture and sprinkle with parsley.

(See picture opposite.)

Stuffed cabbage *(see page 71)*

Cauliflower Polonaise

1 medium-sized cauliflower
salt
2 oz butter

2 oz fresh white breadcrumbs
1 egg, hard-boiled and sieved
1 tbsp chopped parsley

Cook the cauliflower in fast-boiling salted water for about 25–30 minutes. Melt 1 oz of the butter in a small pan and add the breadcrumbs. Cook until golden, stirring frequently, then mix with the sieved egg and parsley. Drain the cauliflower and arrange on a serving plate, melt the remaining 1 oz butter and when it is on the point of turning brown, pour it over the cauliflower. Sprinkle with the breadcrumb mixture and serve at once.

(See picture on page 76.)

Celery with tomatoes

1 head of celery (about $\frac{3}{4}$ lb)
salt
1 lb firm red tomatoes

1 oz butter
pinch of dried tarragon
black pepper

Trim the celery and wash thoroughly, scrubbing the stems if necessary; slice thickly. Cook in boiling salted water until tender—about 20 minutes. Drain thoroughly. Skin and quarter the tomatoes. To the celery pan add the butter. When melted, add the tarragon, then the cooked celery and tomato quarters. Cover and cook over a slow heat for about 5 minutes, shaking the pan occasionally. Add the coarsely ground pepper.

Courgettes

Cook these mini-marrows unpeeled, leaving them whole or cut into $\frac{1}{2}$ in. rounds. Blanch them whole or thickly sliced in salted water for 5 minutes, then drain, and finish by baking, sautéing, frying or stuffing. Add chopped parsley or tarragon when serving as a main course accompaniment.

Courgettes Creole

2 lb courgettes
1 tbsp cooking oil
2–3 spring onions, chopped

salt and pepper
15-oz can of tomatoes

Wash the courgettes, top and tail them and slice diagonally, $\frac{1}{2}$ in. thick. Heat the oil and sauté the spring onions. Add the courgettes, salt and pepper and simmer over a low heat for 10 minutes. Add the tomatoes and simmer for 5 minutes longer.

Stuffed courgettes

4 courgettes
3 tbsps cooking oil
4 oz onions, skinned and finely chopped
3 oz green peppers, seeded and chopped

12 oz lean beef, minced
small clove of garlic, skinned
1 lb small tomatoes, skinned
salt and pepper
5-fl. oz carton of soured cream
1 egg yolk

Wipe the courgettes and slice in half along their length. Scoop out the seeds and brush the insides with 1 tbsp of the oil. Bake at 375°F (mark 5) for 20 minutes. Fry the onion and pepper in 2 tbsps oil until tender, then stir in the mince and garlic and cook for 5 minutes longer. Roughly chop half the tomatoes and add to the mixture in the pan. Season with salt and pepper, then finely slice the remaining tomatoes. Blend the cream and egg yolk together. Fill the courgettes with meat filling, laying slices of tomato along the length of each. Spoon the soured cream over and return the dish to the oven for a further ½ hour.

Cucumber

Try cooking cucumber for a change, and serving it with a white sauce, or with melted butter. To cook, peel and cut in half lengthwise, then into pieces about 2 in. long (or dice it), and simmer gently in butter in a covered pan for 10–15 minutes.

Cucumber cups

1 large cucumber
4 oz cooked ham
2 oz mature Cheddar cheese, grated
pinch of mixed herbs

1 level tbsp tomato paste
1 oz butter, melted
paprika

Thinly pare the rind from the cucumber; cut the cucumber into 12 equal-sized pieces and blanch in boiling salted water for 10 minutes. Drain and refresh under cold running water. Chop the ham finely, put in a bowl with the cheese, herbs and tomato paste and blend together.

Remove the centre from each cucumber with an apple corer. Brush an ovenproof dish with a little butter and arrange the cucumber cups sitting upright, in a single layer. Spoon ham filling into the centre of each piece of cucumber. Brush with melted butter, cover with kitchen foil or a lid, and bake in the oven at 400°F (mark 6) for about 20 minutes. Add paprika and serve.

Kohl rabi

This vegetable has a stem enlarged to a turnip-like globe which grows above the ground, topped with curly green leaves. Eat the enlarged stems while they are small and young. To prepare kohl rabi, cut off the leaves and peel thickly; leave the globes whole if they are small; otherwise cut them into thick slices or cubes. Cook in boiling water until soft—for $\frac{1}{2}$–1 hour, according to size—and serve with a white sauce, or with butter and chopped parsley.

Leek and bacon upside-down

8 oz long-grain American rice
1 oz butter
1 lb leeks

$\frac{1}{2}$ lb streaky bacon rashers
salt and pepper
2 hard-boiled eggs, sliced

Cook the rice in just sufficient salted water to be absorbed in the cooking time. Stir in the butter and keep warm. Thinly slice the leeks and wash thoroughly; blanch in boiling water for 5 minutes and drain. Rind and dice the bacon; fry the rashers until the fat starts to flow and the bacon is lightly browned. Stir in the leeks and cook for a few minutes longer. Adjust the seasoning.

Gently fold the sliced eggs through the leek mixture. Turn it into a buttered $2\frac{1}{2}$-pint tin or dish, such as a casserole or pudding basin. Top with buttered rice, pressing down lightly. Cover with foil and heat through in the oven at 350°F (mark 4) for 15 minutes. Invert on to a warm serving dish. If you wish, serve a thin cheese sauce with this dish.

(See picture below, right.)

Marrows

Large marrows must be peeled and seeded and the flesh cut into even-sized pieces. Cook in boiling salted water until soft, then drain well and serve with a white, tomato or cheese sauce poured over. Marrow can also be roasted in the dripping round the meat, or stuffed and baked—either whole or in rings.

Left: Cauliflower Polonaise *(see page 74)*. Right: Leek and bacon upside down *(see above)*

Tossing a salad in an oil and vinegar dressing *(see page 69)*

Marrow and tomato bake

½ a vegetable marrow, peeled, seeded, and cubed
salt and pepper
½ lb tomatoes, skinned

½ pint cheese sauce
toast triangles
parsley to garnish

(Serves 3–4)

Grease a casserole and put in the cubed marrow, with salt and pepper. Cover and cook gently in the oven at 325°F (mark 3) until the marrow is almost tender. Drain off any surplus liquid, add the quartered tomatoes and the cheese sauce. Leave the lid off to brown the top, and serve with the toast triangles and the parsley garnish.

Mushrooms

Make the most of the different kinds of mushrooms. Use button mushrooms in white sauce or serve whole; or slice them and have them raw in a crisp salad. Those which are slightly riper and starting to open—mushroom cups—are excellent for slicing and adding to soups and stews, or for using whole for baking and stuffing. Flat mushrooms are the ones to use for grilling and frying. Most of the mushrooms bought today are cultivated and require only wiping or washing and draining before being used. Field mushrooms need skinning and should be thoroughly washed to remove any mud or grit.

Stuffed mushrooms

8 medium-sized open mushrooms,
  washed and drained
1 small onion, skinned and
  finely chopped
½ oz butter or margarine
3 tbsps finely chopped ham or
  cooked bacon

5 tbsps fresh breadcrumbs
1 oz cheese, grated
1 tsp chopped parsley
beaten egg
salt and pepper
4 slices of toast, buttered

Remove and chop the stalks from the mushrooms. Lightly fry the mushroom stalks and onion in the butter for 3–5 minutes until soft but not coloured. Add the ham or bacon, breadcrumbs, cheese and parsley and enough egg to bind them all together. Stir until well mixed and hot; season to taste and pile into the mushroom caps. Put the mushrooms in a greased tin, cover with greaseproof paper or foil and bake in the centre of the oven at 375°F (mark 5) for about 20 minutes. Serve on buttered toast.

Meat-stuffed onions

6 large onions, skinned
salt and pepper
½ lb pork, minced
¾ lb pie veal, minced

1 level tsp dried thyme
grated rind of ½ a lemon
1 egg, beaten
a little cooking oil

(Serves 4–6)

Cook the onions in boiling salted water for ½–¾ hour, according to size. Drain them, and carefully ease out the centres. Mix together the pork, veal, thyme, lemon rind, egg and some seasoning. Place the onions in a greased ovenproof casserole, then stuff each with meat mixture. Brush the onions with oil, cover and bake at 375°F (mark 5) for 40–50 minutes. Serve immediately.

Onion and apple open tart

1 lb cooking apples
1–2 onions, parboiled
4 oz shortcrust pastry
  (4 oz plain flour, etc.)
4 oz cheese, grated

2 eggs
½ pint milk
salt and pepper
tomatoes (optional)

Peel, core and slice the apples; chop the onions. Put the apples and onions into a pan with a very little water and simmer gently until tender. Line a pie-plate with the pastry, put in the cooled apple and onion mixture and sprinkle with the cheese. Beat the eggs and pour on the milk; season and pour over the filling. Bake towards the top of the oven at 425°F (mark 7) for 10 minutes to brown the pastry, then at 350°F (mark 4) for a further 20–30 minutes till the custard is set. Slices of tomato may be placed over the top about halfway through the baking time. Serve either hot or cold.

Parsnips

These are delicious when roasted round the joint for about 1 hour. Parboil them first for 5 minutes in salted water, drain well and place round the meat in the baking tin, or in a separate tin into a little hot dripping. Or boil them, then cut into rounds about ½ in. thick; when cold, dip in batter and fry until golden-brown.

Peas à la Française

¼ of a lettuce, washed and shredded
   finely
6 spring onions, halved and trimmed
2–3 sprigs of mint and parsley, tied
   together
1½ lb peas, shelled

¼ pint water
1 oz butter
salt and pepper
2 level tsps sugar
butter for serving

Put all the ingredients except the butter in a saucepan, cover closely and simmer until cooked—about 25 minutes. Remove the parsley and mint, drain the peas well and serve with a knob of butter.

Sauté of peas

2 lb peas, shelled
1 oz butter
2 small onions, skinned and sliced

about ½ pint light stock
salt and pepper
1 tsp chopped parsley

Sauté the peas in the butter for about 2 minutes and add the onions, and just enough stock to cover the peas. Season with salt and pepper, cover and cook gently until soft—about 25 minutes. Don't drain, but serve the liquid with the peas. If liked, the lid can be removed about 10 minutes before the end of the cooking time, so that some of the water evaporates. Sprinkle the chopped parsley on just before serving.

Potatoes

Next time you serve mashed potato, try adding a little chopped watercress (about 1 tbsp to 1 lb) or freshly chopped mint (1 tsp to 1 lb of potatoes); either flavouring is suitable to serve with lamb dishes. And a good accompaniment for sausages is scalloped or oven-cooked potato and onion; slice the peeled potatoes thinly and arrange them in layers in a greased ovenproof dish, sprinkling each layer with salt, pepper and finely minced onion. Barely cover with milk and bake at 325°F (mark 3), until the top is browned and the potatoes are cooked.

Baked stuffed potatoes

Choose even-sized old potatoes; scrub well and dry. Prick all over with a fork. Bake near the top of a fairly hot oven—400°F (mark 6)—for about ¾–1 hour for small potatoes, 1–1¼ hours for large ones, or until they feel soft when pinched. Cut in halves lengthwise and scoop out the centres, taking care to keep the skins intact. Mash the potato in a basin and add one of the stuffings listed here. (These quantities are sufficient for 4 potatoes.) Mix well, pile back into the skins and fork the tops. Sprinkle with cheese or brush with a little milk and return to the oven until hot and golden-brown.

1 3 oz cheese, grated   a little milk
    1 oz butter   salt, pepper and grated nutmeg

2 3 oz bacon, chopped and fried   salt and pepper
    a little milk

3 3 oz smoked haddock, cooked and   1 tsp lemon juice
       mashed   a little milk
    1 tsp chopped parsley   salt, pepper and grated nutmeg

4 2–3 tbsps cream   salt
    2 tsps chopped chives

Chicken-filled sweet peppers *(see page 82)*

Scalloped potatoes and meat

$1\frac{1}{2}$ lb potatoes, peeled
1 small onion, skinned and sliced
$\frac{1}{2}$ lb leftover meat, bacon or ham,
    cubed
$\frac{1}{2}$ pint milk

2 tsps chopped parsley
salt and pepper
$\frac{1}{4}$ level tsp dry mustard
1 oz butter
paprika, to garnish

Parboil the potatoes for 7 minutes, drain and slice. Layer the potatoes, onion and meat in a 3-pint casserole, finishing with potatoes. Blend the milk with the parsley, seasonings and mustard and pour over the potatoes. Dot with the butter, cover and bake in the centre of the oven at 325°F (mark 3) for about $1\frac{1}{2}$ hours. Remove the lid for the last $\frac{1}{2}$ hour in order to brown the potatoes. Garnish with a little paprika.

Spinach with cheese

$1\frac{1}{2}$ lb spinach
salt
$\frac{1}{2}$ oz butter

1 egg yolk
1–2 oz cheese, finely grated

(Serves 3)

Wash the spinach thoroughly and cook in a pan with a little salt but no additional water. When it is tender, drain it thoroughly in a colander and chop with a sharp knife. Put the butter into the pan and add the spinach; toss in the butter, then add the egg yolk and grated cheese. Mix well and serve at once, without further heating.

Spinach quiche

8 oz shortcrust pastry
    (8 oz plain flour, etc.)
$\frac{1}{2}$ lb prepared spinach
water
seasoning

knob of butter
$\frac{1}{2}$ pint single cream
4 egg yolks
4 oz cream cheese

Place 6 4-in. plain flan rings on baking sheets. Divide the pastry into 6 pieces and roll each to fit a flan ring. 'Knock up' the edges. Make sure there are no air pockets between metal and pastry.

In a small saucepan cook the spinach in a little water with salt, pepper and butter. When tender, drain very thoroughly; cool. Divide the spinach between the uncooked pastry cases. Beat together the cream, egg yolks and cheese; season to taste. Spoon evenly over the spinach. Bake in the centre of the oven at 400°F (mark 6) for 10 minutes. Reduce the heat to 350°F (mark 4) and cook for a further 20–25 minutes until the pastry is beginning to colour and the filling lightly set. Serve warm.

Swedes

Mash these after cooking in boiling, salted water with pepper, grated nutmeg and butter; or parboil, then roast them in chunks or fingers, around the joint. Swedes mashed with beaten egg, salt and pepper, and allowed to get cold, can be formed into croquettes, then breadcrumbed and fried.

Chicken-filled sweet peppers

1¼ lb cooked chicken flesh
1½ oz butter or margarine
¼ lb lean streaky bacon, rinded and diced
4 oz onion, skinned and roughly chopped
¼ lb button mushrooms, trimmed
½ level tsp dried thyme

1 level tsp paprika
½ pint chicken stock
2 level tbsps cornflour
2 tbsps water
¼ pint single cream
6 large green peppers
salt and freshly ground black pepper
8 oz long-grain rice

(Serves 6)

Cut the chicken flesh into strips. Melt 1 oz butter and sauté the bacon and onion for 5 minutes. Add the remaining butter and the mushrooms and sauté for 5 minutes longer. Stir in the thyme, paprika and ½ pint stock. Blend the cornflour with the water and pour into the bubbling juices, stirring. Remove pan from the heat, add the cream and gently reheat. Add the chicken and adjust the seasoning.

Blanch the whole peppers in boiling water for 5 minutes, then drain. Cut off the tops, scoop out the seeds and spoon the chicken mixture into the peppers. Lightly cover with buttered foil and cook in the oven at 325°F (mark 3) for about ½ hour. Serve with boiled rice.

(See picture on page 80.)

Sweetcorn

Make the most of the corn-on-the-cob when in season (although you can, of course, get it all the year round frozen or in cans, on the cob and in kernels). The whole fresh corn is simply boiled in unsalted water (salt at this stage makes the kernels tough) for 12–20 minutes, and served with melted butter, salt and freshly ground pepper. It's ideal for children's suppers and lunches and they will enjoy eating them in their fingers. Provide paper napkins for buttery hands. If you mount each corn cob on a pair of metal holders designed for the purpose, it is much less messy to tackle.

Frozen sweetcorn can be 'dressed up' by tossing the kernels, after cooking them lightly, in 2 tbsps double cream. Or add a few slices of red and green peppers which have been simmered for 10 minutes to the cooked kernels and add a knob of butter.

Sweetcorn special

3 large eggs
medium-sized can of sweetcorn
3 oz margarine

salt and pepper
3 large tomatoes
3 oz Lancashire cheese, grated

Put the eggs to hard-boil. Heat the sweetcorn in a saucepan with 2 oz margarine and some seasoning for 3 minutes. Halve the tomatoes, dot with the rest of the margarine and grill for 5 minutes. Drain and shell the eggs. Drain the sweetcorn and pour into an ovenproof dish. Halve the hot eggs lengthwise and arrange down the centre of the dish, on top of the sweetcorn. Season, cover with cheese and brown for 4 minutes under the grill. Put the tomatoes round the edge of the dish, garnish with parsley and serve at once.

Baked stuffed tomatoes

4 even-sized tomatoes
1 oz ham, chopped
1 tsp chopped onion
½ oz butter

2 level tbsps fresh breadcrumbs
½ tsp chopped parsley
2 level tbsps grated cheese (optional)
salt and pepper

Cut a small round from each tomato at the end opposite to the stalk. Scoop out the centres. Lightly fry the ham and onion in the butter for 3 minutes. Add the crumbs, parsley, cheese (if used), the pulp removed from the tomatoes and seasoning. Well fill the tomatoes with this mixture and put on the lids. Bake in the centre of the oven for about 15 minutes at 400°F (mark 6).

Watercress soup

4 oz butter
2 oz plain flour
1¼ pints chicken or veal stock
½ pint milk

salt and freshly ground black pepper
3 oz onion, skinned and chopped
2 bunches of watercress

(Serves 6)

Melt 3 oz butter in a pan, stir in the flour and cook over a gentle heat for 1–2 minutes. Remove from the heat and stir in all the stock and milk. Return to the heat, bring to the boil, stirring continuously and simmer gently for 3 minutes. Season well. Sauté the onion in the remaining butter until soft. Wash the watercress; trim, leaving some of the stem. Retain a few leaves for garnish. Chop roughly and add to the onion, cover with a lid and sauté for a further 4 minutes. Stir the sautéed vegetables into the sauce, then blend in a liquidiser, or pass through a sieve. Gently reheat the soup and season to taste. Serve garnished with watercress leaves.

(See picture on page 84.)

Left: Watercress soup *(see page 83)*. Right: Bubble and squeak bake *(see opposite)*

Below: The main ingredients for Ratatouille *(see page 26)* are amongst this medley of vegetables

Yams (sweet potatoes)

These are not related to ordinary potatoes. They look like turnips, but have a sweet, slightly perfumed flesh, and can be boiled or roasted. Good baked at 400°F (mark 7) for $\frac{1}{2}$ hour and served with roast pork or bacon joint. They can also be served as a sweet; cook them with sugar and add cinnamon.

MISCELLANEOUS VEGETABLE DISHES
Moussaka

2 lb aubergines, trimmed and thinly sliced
salt
8–10 tbsps olive oil
2 oz butter
3 medium-sized onions, skinned and thinly sliced
2 lb raw lean lamb, minced

$2\frac{1}{2}$-oz can of tomato paste
seasoning
15-oz can of plum tomatoes
a bay leaf
1 pint cheese sauce
a little Parmesan cheese, grated
chopped parsley, for garnish

(Serves 6)

Spread out the aubergines in a large plate or tray, sprinkle with salt and leave for at least an hour. Pour off the liquid which collects, and dry the slices with absorbent kitchen paper. Fry the aubergines in batches in the oil for about 10 minutes, turning them frequently. Meanwhile, melt the butter in another pan and sauté the onion until soft. Place the minced lamb in a bowl and stir in the tomato paste and seasoning. Pass the plum tomatoes with their juice through a sieve, or purée them in an electric blender.

In a large ovenproof casserole, arrange layers of aubergine, lamb and onion, adding the bay leaf and finishing with aubergine. Pour the tomato purée over (there should be enough room left for the cheese sauce). Cover and cook in the oven at 350°F (mark 4) for 1 hour. Pour the cheese sauce over the moussaka and sprinkle with a little Parmesan cheese. Replace it in the oven and cook uncovered for about a further $\frac{1}{2}$ hour, until the sauce is golden. Serve sprinkled with chopped parsley.

Bubble and squeak bake

2 lb old potatoes, peeled
butter
milk
salt and pepper

1 lb firm green cabbage
$\frac{1}{2}$ lb onions, skinned
$\frac{1}{2}$ lb carrots, peeled
6 oz mature Cheddar cheese, grated

Cook the potatoes in boiling salted water until tender. Drain, and cream with a knob of butter and a little milk; season well. Meanwhile, cook the cabbage, drain well and chop. Chop the onions finely and grate the carrots; turn them into the boiling salted water, cook for 5 minutes, then drain. Blend the cabbage and potato together. Turn half the mixture into a buttered shallow baking dish 9-in. in diameter (1¾ pints). Cover with onion and carrot and top with 4 oz grated cheese, spread evenly. Top with the remainder of the potato mixture, smooth the surface with a knife, mark with a fork, and sprinkle the remainder of the cheese over the top. Bake in the oven at 400°F (mark 6) for about 40 minutes, until golden-brown. Serve cut in wedges.

(See picture on page 84.)

Top-crust vegetable pie

½ lb onions, skinned
½ lb leeks, trimmed
½ lb carrots, peeled
½ lb turnips, peeled
3 oz butter or margarine
¼ pint water
about ¾ pint milk
½ lb tomatoes, skinned

15½-oz can of butter beans
salt and pepper
2 tbsps chopped parsley
1½ oz flour
6 oz mature Cheddar cheese, grated
8 oz shortcrust pastry
(8 oz flour, etc.)

Chop the onions roughly. Leave some green on the leeks, cut into ¼-in. slices and wash thoroughly. Cut the carrots into matchsticks. Dice the turnips. Melt 1½ oz butter in a pan, add these vegetables and 'sweat' them in the fat, covered with a lid, for 10 minutes. Add the water and simmer for a further 10 minutes. Drain the vegetables and make the juices up to ¾ pint with milk.

Arrange the sweated vegetables in layers with the halved tomatoes and drained butter beans in a 3½-pint pie-dish, adding seasoning between the layers. Add the parsley. If necessary, place a pie funnel among the vegetables.

Put the remaining butter in a clean pan. When melted, stir in the flour and cook for 1–2 minutes. Remove from the heat and gradually beat in milk. Bring to the boil and boil for 1–2 minutes. Stir in the cheese, adjust the seasoning and pour over the vegetables. When the filling is nearly cold, cover with a pastry lid. Place on a baking sheet and bake at 400°F (mark 6) for about ¾ hour.

SALADS

Asparagus and corn salad

2 corn cobs
1 bundle of asparagus, cooked
1 tbsp chopped capers
¼ pint mayonnaise

1 lettuce, prepared
1 hard-boiled egg, sliced
2 tomatoes, sliced

Cook and drain the corn, remove from the cobs and allow to cool. Cut off and discard the woody ends of the asparagus; keep a few heads for garnishing, and put the remainder in a basin with the corn and capers. Add mayonnaise and blend well. Pile into individual salad dishes and garnish with lettuce, sliced egg and tomato.

Avocado Bermuda-style

1 small, 2-oz onion, skinned and
   finely chopped
2 oranges
5 tbsps thick mayonnaise
grated rind of $\frac{1}{2}$ orange

juice of $\frac{1}{2}$ orange
salt and freshly milled black pepper
1 avocado
lemon juice
a bunch of watercress, prepared

Separate the onion into rings. Peel the orange free of all white pith, catching the juice over a basin. In a small bowl combine the mayonnaise, grated orange rind and juice. Adjust the seasoning to taste. Halve, stone and peel the avocado. Thickly slice, crosswise, then cut each slice into 2 chunky pieces. Toss in lemon juice and drain.

Arrange tiny bunches of watercress sprigs on 4 side plates. Top with a few rings of onion; on each side arrange orange slices and fill the middle with the avocado. Spoon orange mayonnaise down the centre over the avocado. Garnish with onion rings and, if you like, very fine strips of orange rind, free of white pith, cut from the discarded orange rind. Prepare shortly before serving; this side salad goes extremely well with golden-crumbed plaice fillets, a plain grilled gammon rasher, succulent veal escalope or cold duck.

Celery and potato salad

1 lb new potatoes
3 spring onions, finely sliced
4 tbsps chopped celery
2 tbsps olive oil

1 tbsp vinegar
salt and pepper
a lettuce heart
a little ham or bacon

Scrub the potatoes and boil them (unpeeled) in salted water until tender; skin, cut into dice and put into a bowl. Mix in the onions and celery. Blend together the olive oil and vinegar and season to taste. Pour this dressing over the vegetables and mix lightly. Line a salad dish with the washed lettuce heart leaves and pile the mixture on top. Add the diced ham or bacon.

Onion and tomato salad

2 onions, skinned and sliced
3 firm tomatoes, skinned and sliced

3–4 tbsps French dressing
chopped chives

Arrange the onions and tomatoes alternately in a shallow dish. Pour the dressing over and serve sprinkled with the chives.

Onion and mint salad

a bunch of spring onions, sliced
a small bunch of mint, chopped
1 level tbsp caster sugar

salt and pepper
vinegar

Arrange the onions and mint layers in a small dish, sprinkling sugar and seasoning between the layers. Add enough vinegar to cover and allow to stand for about 30 minutes before serving. Delicious with cold lamb.

Raisin and nut salad

2 sharp dessert apples
4 oz seeded raisins, chopped
2 oz walnuts, chopped

salad dressing
bunch of watercress, washed and
    trimmed

Wipe the apples; don't peel them, but grate on a clean grater into a basin. Add the chopped raisins and nuts and a little salad dressing and mix lightly. Arrange the watercress in a circle on a plate and pile the fruit mixture in the centre.

Summer salad bowl

1 lettuce
2 avocados
lemon juice

2 heads of chicory
1 box mustard and cress
French dressing

(Serves 4–6)

Prepare lettuce; reserve a few good-looking leaves, and tear the remainder into manageable pieces. Halve, stone and peel the avocados; slice across and sprinkle with lemon juice. Trim and finely slice the chicory. Trim the cress, keeping it in small clusters. Arrange the salad in a deep bowl and dress it just before serving.

Winter salad

2 eating apples, cored and chopped
4 sticks of celery, scrubbed and
    chopped
1 medium-sized cooked beetroot,
    peeled and diced

$\frac{1}{2}$ a small onion, skinned and finely
    chopped
salad cream to bind
a few chopped walnuts, optional

Mix the apples, celery, beetroot and onion and add sufficient salad cream to bind together. Pile on to a dish and serve sprinkled with the chopped walnuts.

5 PUDDINGS AND CAKES

Regardless of motherly concern for their sugar consumption, many children and even some husbands consider the sweet course the best part of the meal. But even a fairly simple pudding seems to take up a disproportionate time to prepare, compared with the more nutritious main course. If your family considers a meal incomplete without one, it is a great help to have a food mixer and blender. Meringues, for instance, equally good for weekend tea or as a dessert, are whisked up in an instant in a mixer, while a blender makes light work of breadcrumbs, biscuit crumbs, fools and other desserts.

Providing variety
One of the simplest ways to provide the variety which is so much appreciated is to ring the changes on a few basic recipes such as baked sponge pudding, steamed pudding, pancakes, and fritters, using fresh, canned and dried fruit. Batch-baking of cakes is another short-cut to variety; a *Victoria sponge* mixture can be adapted in innumerable ways, all looking and tasting different. If you have a freezer you can store a large batch of cakes and pastries to ease the work during the holidays.

Sweet and simple
Pies: Try crumb crust in place of shortcrust. Ready-made pie fillings are rarely sufficient for a family-size pie, but can be stretched with more cooked fruit. They are also useful for upside-down puddings, and make a good sauce for vanilla ice cream.

Milk Puddings: Beat a couple of eggs into the milk and add a few ounces of sultanas and raisins before baking. Pour a dessertspoonful of blackcurrant purée or syrup, or raspberry vinegar, over plain milk pudding.

Jellies: A jelly will go further if you add a can of fruit; make up the jelly with the juice (plus water if necessary to make up to a pint) and fold in the chopped fruit. Or make the jelly rather more stiffly than usual, and when it starts to set, whisk the contents of a chilled can (small) of evaporated milk, and add the jelly. Whisk together until pale and fluffy.

Jellied Fruit Cubes: Popular for a children's party. Make up a jelly as usual, but pour it into a divided ice-cube tray, having first put a piece of fruit or a cherry in each division. When set, remove the divisions and serve the squares piled up with ice cream in individual glasses.

Meringue Fillings: For tea-time, use flavoured buttercream sometimes in place of fresh cream to sandwich them together. For dessert, serve with ice cream, fruit, or pie filling. Or add finely chopped nuts or melted chocolate to whipped cream (for special occasions, adults may prefer the addition of a little brandy or liqueur).

HOT PUDDINGS

Steamed sponge pudding

4 oz butter or margarine
4 oz caster sugar
2 eggs, beaten

a few drops of vanilla essence
6 oz self-raising flour
a little milk, to mix

Use a steamer or large saucepan and put in enough water to come halfway up the sides; put it on to boil. Grease a 1½-pint pudding basin. Cream together the fat and sugar until pale and fluffy, then add the egg and the vanilla essence, a little at a time, beating well after each addition. Using a metal spoon, fold in half the sifted flour, with enough milk to give a dropping consistency, then fold in the rest. Put the mixture into the basin, cover with buttered greaseproof paper or foil and secure with string or elastic. Steam for 1½ hours, topping up the water when necessary. Serve with jam sauce.

This basic pudding recipe can be adapted in various ways to give variety and suit individual tastes.

Variations

Syrup Sponge Pudding: Put 2 level tbsps golden syrup into the bottom of the basin before adding the mixture. (See picture on page 92.)

Fruit Sponge Pudding: Put a layer of drained canned fruit, or a layer of stewed fruit, in the basin before adding the mixture.

Mincemeat Surprise Pudding: Line the bottom and sides of the basin with a thin layer of mincemeat and fill with the pudding mixture. When the pudding is cooked, turn it out carefully so that the outside remains completely covered with the mincemeat. Sometimes known as Mock Christmas Pudding, this makes a less rich alternative to the traditional version.

Jamaica Pudding: Add 2–4 oz chopped preserved ginger with the flour. Serve with a syrup sauce.

Cherry Sponge: Add 2–3 oz halved glacé cherries with the flour. Serve with custard or sweet white sauce.

Note: Remember when steaming puddings to keep the water in the steamer boiling rapidly all the time; have a kettle of boiling water ready to top it up regularly.

Baked sponge

3 oz butter or margarine
3 oz caster sugar
1 egg, beaten

5 oz self-raising flour
$\frac{1}{2}$ tsp vanilla essence
a little milk to mix

Grease a 1$\frac{1}{2}$-pint ovenproof dish. Cream the fat and sugar until pale and fluffy. Add the egg a little at a time, beating after each addition. Fold in the flour with the essence and a little milk, to give a dropping consistency. Put into a prepared dish and bake towards the top of the oven at 350°F (mark 4) for 30–40 minutes, until well risen and golden. Serve with syrup sauce or custard.

Variations

Jam Sponge: Put 2–3 tbsps jam in a layer over the bottom of the dish before adding the sponge mixture.

Baked Castle Puddings: Grease 8 individual foil dishes or dariole moulds and put 1–2 tsps jam in each. Divide the mixture between the dishes, bake for 20 minutes and serve with jam sauce.

Orange or Lemon Sponge: Grate and squeeze an orange or a lemon. Add the rind to the creamed mixture and replace the milk by the juice. Serve with an orange or lemon sauce.

Spicy Fruit Sponge: Sift $\frac{1}{2}$–1 level tsp mixed spice with the flour. Add 3–4 oz sultanas or currants and 1–2 oz chopped glacé cherries, or cut mixed peel, with the flour. Serve with white sauce or custard.

Chocolate Sponge: Add 1 oz cocoa, sifted with the flour, or stir 1 oz chocolate dots into the mixture. Serve with chocolate sauce.

Steamed suet pudding

6 oz self-raising flour
a pinch of salt
3 oz shredded suet

2 oz caster sugar
about $\frac{1}{4}$ pint milk

Mix the flour, salt, suet and sugar. Make a well in the centre and add enough milk to give a soft, dropping consistency. Put into a greased 1$\frac{1}{2}$-pint pudding basin, cover with buttered greaseproof paper or foil and secure with string or elastic. Steam over rapidly boiling water for 1$\frac{1}{2}$–2 hours. Serve with a jam, golden syrup, or fruit sauce.

Variations

For a lighter pudding, use 3 oz self-raising flour and 3 oz fresh breadcrumbs. For a richer version, use 1 beaten egg and about 6 tbsps milk in place of the $\frac{1}{4}$ pint milk.

Jam Suet Pudding: Put 2 level tbsps red jam in the greased basin before adding the mixture.

Apple Suet Pudding: Add to the dry ingredients $\frac{1}{2}$ lb cooking apples, peeled and finely chopped or grated. Serve the pudding with a sweet white sauce flavoured with a pinch of nutmeg.

Date Suet Pudding: Add 4 oz chopped dates and the grated rind of a lemon, and reduce the sugar to 1 oz. Serve with lemon sauce.

Pancakes

4 oz plain flour
a pinch of salt

1 egg
$\frac{1}{2}$ pint milk or milk and water

Sift the flour and salt into a bowl, make a well in the centre and break in the egg. Add half the liquid and beat the mixture until smooth. Add the remaining liquid gradually and beat until well mixed. Heat a little lard in a frying-pan until really hot, running it round to coat the sides of the pan;

Syrup sponge pudding *(see page 90)*

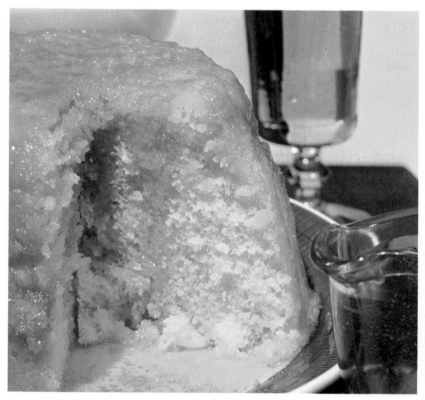

pour off any surplus. Pour or spoon in just enough batter to cover the base of the pan thinly and cook quickly, until golden-brown underneath. Turn with a palette knife, or by tossing, and cook the second side until golden-brown. Turn out on to sugared paper, sprinkle with sugar and a squeeze of lemon juice and serve at once, with extra sugar and lemon wedges.

If you are cooking a large number of pancakes, keep them warm by putting them as they are made between two plates in a warm oven. When ready to dish up, place filling (if required) in the centre, roll them up and serve immediately.

Variations

Jam Pancakes: Spread the pancakes with jam, roll them up and serve with cream.

Orange Pancakes: Add the grated rind of an orange to the batter and cook in the usual way. To serve, sprinkle with sugar and pour the orange juice over them.

Ginger and Banana Pancakes: Add 1 level tsp powdered ginger with the flour and cook the pancakes as usual. For the filling, mash 1 banana per person with double cream and add some small pieces of preserved ginger. Spread the filling on the cooked pancakes, roll them up and serve with whipped cream.

Layered Pancakes: Instead of rolling the pancakes, use a filling, such as whipped cream and jam, to layer the pancakes one on top of the other. The layered pancake is served cut in wedges like a cake.

Surprise Pancakes: Make the pancakes as usual, then spoon some ice cream into the centre of each pancake and fold in half, like an omelette. Serve at once with jam sauce, or a sauce made from sieved raspberries.

Fruit fritters *(see page 94)*

Fruit fritters

4 oz plain flour
a pinch of salt
1 egg

$\frac{1}{4}$ pint of milk or milk and water
fat, for deep-frying

For the filling

3–4 cooking apples, peeled, cored and
cut in rings $\frac{1}{4}$-in. thick
or, a few canned pineapple rings

or, 4 small bananas, peeled and cut in
half lengthwise.

Make a well in the centre of the sifted flour and salt and break in the egg.
Add half the liquid and beat the mixture until smooth. Gradually add the
rest of the liquid and beat again. Heat the fat until it is hot enough to brown a
1-in. cube of bread in 60–70 seconds.

Dip the prepared fruit in the batter and fry until golden. Drain on
crumpled kitchen paper, toss in caster sugar and a little powdered cinnamon,
and serve immediately.

(See picture on page 93.)

Applescotch flan

8 oz shortcrust pastry
(8 oz plain flour, etc.)
4 oz golden syrup
1 large egg

1 lb cooking apples, peeled, cored
and sliced
1 oz butter

Line a shallow tin, 12-in. by $7\frac{1}{2}$-in. with the pastry. Beat together the
golden syrup and egg. Pour half the syrup over the pastry base. Arrange
the apple slices on top and pour over the remainder of the syrup. Dot
with tiny pieces of butter. Bake at 400°F (mark 6) in the centre of the oven
for about $\frac{3}{4}$ hour. Serve with whipped cream or ice cream.

Lemon bombe pudding

8 oz self-raising flour
a pinch of salt
4 oz shredded suet

6 oz soft brown sugar
1 large thin-skinned lemon,
washed and dried

Sift the flour with the salt and add the suet. Stir in sufficient water to
make a soft, but manageable, dough. Line a greased $1\frac{1}{2}$-pint pudding basin
with the pastry, reserving a piece for the lid. Put enough of the soft brown
sugar into the lined basin to come halfway up the sides. Put the lemon,
whole, in the centre and fill up with more sugar. Damp the edges of the pastry
and cover with the pastry lid, rolled to fit. Cover in the usual way for a
steamed pudding and place in a saucepan with water reaching halfway up.
Boil gently for 4 hours.

This hearty, fruit-flavoured pudding produces its own delicious sauce.
Some people eat the lemon, others don't.

Queen of puddings

¾ pint milk
1 oz butter
2½ oz caster sugar
3 oz fresh white breadcrumbs

2 large eggs, separated
grated rind 1 lemon
2 tbsps strawberry, raspberry or
    apricot jam

Warm the milk in a saucepan with the butter and 1 oz sugar, and add the breadcrumbs. Remove from heat and add the beaten egg yolks and lemon rind; pour into a greased 2-pint pie-dish. Cook in the oven at 350°F (mark 4) for about 20 minutes until just set. Take out and spread the surface lightly with jam. Whisk the egg whites stiffly and fold in 1 oz sugar. Spread the meringue mixture on top of the jam and dredge with a little more sugar. Replace in the oven and bake at 300°F (mark 1–2) for a further ¾–1 hour until meringue is crisp and tipped with brown.

    An unusual variation to this classic recipe is to use 3 oz ginger cake crumbs and honey instead of white breadcrumbs and jam.

Aunt Moll's bread pudding

8 oz stale bread
4 oz currants, raisins or sultanas
2 oz brown sugar
2 oz shredded suet

1 oz chopped mixed peel
1 level tsp mixed spice
1 egg, beaten
a little milk

(Serves 4–6)

Break the bread into small pieces and soak in cold water for at least ½ hour, then strain it and squeeze as dry as possible. Put into a basin and beat out the lumps with a fork. Add the dried fruit, sugar, suet, peel and mixed spice. Mix well. Add the beaten egg and enough milk to form a dropping consistency. Turn into a greased 7-in. round cake tin or a 2-pint pie-dish. Bake in the oven at 325°F (mark 3) for 1–1½ hours. To serve, turn out on to a warm dish and dredge with sugar. Serve with custard or lemon sauce.

Spiced semolina pudding

1 pint milk
1½ oz semolina
3 oz sugar
1–2 level tsps mixed spice

grated rind of ½ a lemon
2 oz currants, sultanas or stoned
    raisins
2 eggs, separated

Heat the milk, sprinkle in the semolina, bring to the boil and cook for 2–3 minutes, stirring all the time. Remove from the heat and stir in half the sugar, the spice, lemon rind, dried fruit and egg yolks. Pour the mixture into an ovenproof dish. Whisk the egg whites stiffly, fold in the remaining sugar, and pile on top of the pudding. Bake towards the top of the oven at 400°F (mark 6) for 5–10 minutes, until the meringue is lightly browned.

Alternatively, you can add all the sugar to the pudding, fold in the whisked egg whites and bake for 15–20 minutes, or until the pudding is well risen and lightly browned.

PIES AND FLANS

Apple and blackberry lattice pie

1½ lb cooking apples, peeled, cored
   and sliced
4 oz sugar
4 tbsps water
(Serves 4–6)

8 oz blackberries
8 oz shortcrust pastry
   (8 oz plain flour, etc.)

In a saucepan cook together the apples, sugar and water until the apples are tender, but not mushy. Leave until cold. Fold the blackberries through the apple mixture.

Stand a 7½-in. fluted flan ring on a baking sheet. Roll out the pastry, reserving a little to line the ring and press firmly into the flutes. Fill with the apple mixture. Roll out the remaining pastry and cut into strips, using a pastry wheel. Arrange lattice-fashion over the fruit, using a little water to fix the strips. Bake in the centre of the oven at 400°F (mark 6) for about ¾ hour, until the pastry is light golden-brown.

Serve warm, not hot, with whipped cream or custard.

Pear and lemon pie

15-oz can pear halves
1 lemon
2 level tbsps cornflour

4½ oz caster sugar
2 eggs, separated
7-in. baked shortcrust flan case

Drain the pears, but reserve the syrup. Chop the flesh roughly. Finely grate the lemon rind and squeeze the juice. In a saucepan blend the cornflour to a cream with the lemon juice, slowly stir in 6 fl. oz pear syrup and add the lemon rind and ½ oz sugar. Bring to the boil, stirring continuously and cook for 1 minute. Remove from the heat, beat in the egg yolks one at a time. Add the chopped pears and fold them gently through, then spread the mixture over the pastry case.

Whisk the egg whites until firm and add half the remaining sugar; continue to beat until stiff and glossy. Fold in the rest of sugar. Spread over the filling and turn into peaks. Bake in the centre of the oven at 350°F (mark 4) for 10–15 minutes until the surface of the meringue is crisp and lightly browned.

Raspberry and banana flan

**8-in. plain-edged baked shortcrust
  flan case**
1 lb bananas
grated rind and juice of 1 lemon

1 level tbsp sugar
15½-oz can raspberries
½ a 1-pint raspberry jelly tablet

(Serves 6)

Make the pastry case. Peel the bananas, toss them lightly in the lemon rind,
1 tbsp lemon juice and the sugar. Mash with a fork and spread the mixture
over the base of the pastry case. Drain the raspberries and reserve juice.
Make up the jelly to ½ pint with the raspberry juice, the rest of the lemon
juice and as much water as is necessary. Cool the jelly until it is of the
consistency of unbeaten egg white. Arrange the drained raspberries over the
banana. When the jelly is on the point of setting, spoon over the fruit and
leave until set.

Lemon rice cream *(see page 98)*

Lemon rice cream

3 oz pudding rice	3 egg yolks
1½ pints milk	powdered cinnamon
1½ oz sugar	caster sugar
the rind of 1 lemon, thinly pared	lemon wedges, to garnish

Wash the rice in cold water and drain well. In a pan, mix the rice, milk, sugar and lemon rind. Cover and cook very slowly over a low heat, stirring occasionally, until thick and creamy—about ¾ hour. Discard the lemon rind and stir in the beaten egg yolks. Reheat, but *do not boil*. Turn into a shallow dish. When cold, but not chilled, decorate with a lattice pattern of cinnamon blended with a little sugar. Serve garnished with lemon wedges.

(See picture on page 97.)

Scandinavian pudding

3 oz wholemeal breadcrumbs	a little caster sugar, to sweeten
1 oz margarine	apples
2 tbsps brown sugar	raspberry jam
1¼ lb cooking apples, peeled, cored and sliced	½ oz grated chocolate

Fry the breadcrumbs in the margarine with the brown sugar. Stew the apples in a very little water to form a smooth pulp and sweeten to taste. Spread a layer of fried breadcrumbs over the base of a greased round dish, reserving enough for the topping, cover with a layer of apples and then add a layer of raspberry jam. Repeat, finishing with the rest of the crumbs; press these firmly into the dish. Leave to cool, then turn out and decorate with grated chocolate.

Rhubarb snow

¾ lb rhubarb, cut in 1-in. pieces	4–6 oz sugar
1 lb cooking apples, peeled, cored and sliced	4 tbsps double cream
thinly grated rind and juice of 1 orange	2 egg whites, stiffly whisked

(Serves 6)

Put the rhubarb and apples in a pan with the orange rind and juice and bring to the boil. Cover and simmer until soft. Stir in the sugar, beat until smooth and then chill. Just before serving, stir in the cream, fold in the egg whites and pile in glasses.

Gooseberry flummery

½ pint milk
2 oz semolina
2 eggs, separated
1½ oz caster sugar

½ pint thick sweetened gooseberry
purée
4 tbsps lemon juice

Heat the milk and shower the semolina into it. Simmer for 10 minutes,
stirring. Add the egg yolks and sugar, and whisk well. Fold the puréed fruit
and lemon juice into the mixture, and then the stiffly-beaten egg whites.
Turn into four sundae glasses and chill.

SAUCES FOR ICE CREAM

Butterscotch sauce

2 oz butter or margarine
2 oz brown sugar
2 level tbsps golden syrup

a squeeze of lemon juice
1 oz chopped nuts, if liked

Warm the butter, sugar and syrup in a saucepan until well blended. Boil
for 1 minute, then stir in the lemon juice. Add the chopped nuts, if used.

Chocolate sauce

4 oz plain chocolate
2 level tbsps golden syrup

4 tbsps evaporated milk

Over a very low heat, melt the chocolate with the syrup and milk but do not
boil. When smooth, increase heat to desired serving temperature.

Chocolate peppermint sauce

8 oz chocolate peppermint creams
6-oz can evaporated milk

1 oz butter

Break up the chocolate creams and put them into a saucepan with the milk.
Stir over a gentle heat until melted. When hot, add butter, stir and serve
immediately.

Coffee-caramel sauce

4 oz caster sugar
2 tbsps water

½ pint strong black coffee

Dissolve the sugar in the water in a thick pan, over gentle heat, without
stirring. Bring to the boil and boil rapidly until golden-brown. Slowly add
the boiling, strong black coffee and stir until the caramel dissolves. Boil for a
few minutes. The flavour of this sauce is best appreciated if it is served while
still warm.

Fudge sauce

½ lb fudge
6-oz can evaporated milk
1 level tsp cornflour

1 tbsp water
a few drops vanilla essence

Heat the fudge and milk together gently in a small, heavy-based saucepan until the fudge softens. Blend the cornflour with the water and stir into the fudge and milk with a few drops of vanilla essence. Bring to the boil, stirring. Leave until cold.

Honey sauce

2 oz butter
1½ level tsps cornflour

4–6 oz thin honey

Melt the butter and stir in the cornflour. Gradually add the honey. Bring to the boil and cook for 1–2 minutes.

Honey and almond sauce

1½ oz butter or margarine
1 oz blanched almonds, shredded
  or flaked

juice of 1 lemon
3 level tbsps thick honey

Melt the butter or margarine in a saucepan, add the almonds and cook gently until browned. Just before serving, add the lemon juice and honey.

Marshmallow sauce

4 oz sugar
3 tbsps water
8 marshmallows, cut up small

1 egg white
½ tsp vanilla essence
a few drops of red colouring, if liked

Dissolve the sugar in the water and boil for 5 minutes. Add the marshmallows and stir until melted. Whip the egg white stiffly and gradually fold in the marshmallow mixture. Flavour with vanilla and tint pink, if desired. Serve over coffee or chocolate ice cream.

Melba sauce

4 level tbsps redcurrant jelly
3 oz sugar
½ lb fresh raspberries or a 15-oz can

2 level tsps arrowroot or cornflour
1 tbsp water

Prepare ¼ pint of raspberry purée. Mix the jelly, sugar and purée and bring to the boil. Blend the arrowroot or cornflour with the cold water to a smooth cream and stir in a little of the raspberry mixture; return the sauce to the pan. Bring to the boil, stirring with a wooden spoon, until it thickens and clears. Strain and serve cold.

Red jam sauce

3 rounded tbsps red jam
¼ pint water or fruit juice
2 level tsps arrowroot or cornflour

2 tbsps water
a squeeze of lemon juice

Warm the jam and water and simmer for 5 minutes. Blend the arrowroot and cold water to a smooth cream and stir in the jam mixture. Return the sauce to the pan and heat, stirring, until it thickens and clears. Add the lemon juice before serving, cold.

For a thicker sauce, simply melt the jam on its own over a gentle heat and add a little lemon juice.

For a quick dessert, there is nothing nicer than fresh fruit and cream

CAKES

Home-made cakes and cookies are so much more delicious than most bought varieties that it is well worthwhile having a regular weekly 'bake'. In these recipes, if using margarine instead of butter, you will find it preferable to use the 'block' type rather than 'soft tub' margarine.

Victoria sponge sandwich

4 oz butter or margarine	4 oz self-raising flour
4 oz caster sugar	1–2 rounded tbsps jam
2 eggs, beaten	caster sugar, to dredge

Grease two 7-in. sandwich tins and line the base of each with a round of buttered greaseproof paper. Cream the fat and sugar until pale and fluffy. Add the egg, a little at a time, beating well after each addition. Fold in half the flour, using a metal spoon, then fold in the rest. Place half the mixture in each tin and level it with a knife. Bake both cakes on the same shelf, in roughly the centre of the oven, at 375°F (mark 5) for about 20 minutes or until they are well risen and golden, firm to the touch and beginning to shrink away from the sides of the tins. When cool, sandwich together with jam and sprinkle the top with caster sugar.

Variations

Chocolate: Replace ½ oz of the flour with 1 oz cocoa. Sandwich together with vanilla or chocolate butter cream.

Orange or Lemon: Add 1–2 level tsps grated orange or lemon rind to the mixture. Sandwich the cakes together with orange or lemon curd, or orange or lemon butter cream; use the juice of the fruit to make glacé icing for the top.

Coffee: Add 2 tsps instant coffee dissolved in a little warm water to the creamed mixture with the egg.

This basic *Victoria sponge sandwich* recipe can be used to bake a slab cake for icing and cutting up into a wide variety of small cakes (see *Small Cakes and Cookies* section of this chapter).

Swiss roll

3 eggs	1 tbsp hot water
4 oz caster sugar	caster sugar, to dredge
4 oz plain flour	some warmed jam

Line a Swiss roll tin 9-in. by 12-in. with buttered greaseproof or 'non-stick' paper. Put the eggs and sugar in a large deep bowl, stand the bowl over a pan of hot water and whisk until light and creamy; the mixture should be stiff enough to retain the impression of the whisk for a few seconds. Remove the bowl from the heat and whisk until cool. Sift half the flour over the mixture and fold in very lightly, using a metal spoon. Add the remaining flour in the same way, and finally lightly stir in the hot water. Pour the mixture into the prepared tin, allowing it to run over the whole surface. Bake near the top of the oven at 425°F (mark 7) for 7–9 minutes until golden-brown, well risen and firm.

Meanwhile, have ready a sheet of greaseproof paper liberally sprinkled with caster sugar. Place this over a tea towel lightly wrung out in hot water; this will help to make the sponge pliable. Turn the cake quickly out on to the paper, trim off the crusty edges with a sharp knife and spread the surface with warmed jam. Roll up the cake with the aid of the paper, making the first turn firmly so that the whole cake will roll evenly and have a good shape when finished; but roll more lightly after the first turn. Dredge with sugar and cool on a cake rack.

Variations

Chocolate Swiss Roll: Replace 1 level tbsp of the flour with 1 level tbsp cocoa. If you are using a cream filling, turn out the cooked sponge and trim as above, but don't spread with the filling immediately. Instead, cover the sponge with a sheet of greaseproof paper and roll it up loosely. When the cake is cold, unroll, remove the paper and spread with cream or butter cream and roll it up again.

Small Swiss Rolls: Bake and trim as above then cut in half lengthways. Spread each half with jam and roll up, starting at the longer sides and make 2 long thin rolls. When the cake is cold, cut each roll into 3 even lengths. These miniature Swiss rolls are always very popular for children's parties.

Coffee marble cake

8 oz butter or margarine
8 oz caster sugar
4 large eggs

8 oz self-raising flour
2 tbsps coffee essence
a little icing sugar

Well grease a 3½-pint fluted or plain ring mould. Beat the fat until soft but not oily. Add the sugar and cream it in until the mixture is light and fluffy. Add the eggs, one at a time, beating between each addition, then lightly beat in the flour. Divide the mixture into two parts, and add the coffee essence to one part. Place the mixtures in alternate spoonfuls into the prepared tin. Level the surface. Swirl through the mixture with a skewer but don't overdo this, as it will spoil the effect. Bake in the centre of the oven at 350°F (mark 4) for about ¾ hour until well risen and spongy to the touch. Turn out on to a wire rack to cool. Serve dusted with icing sugar.

(See picture on page 113.)

Left: Yacht birthday cake *(see page 106)*. Right: Cup cakes *(see page 108)*

Gingerbread

8 oz plain flour
½ level tsp salt
1½ level tsps ground ginger
1½ level tsps baking powder
4 oz Demerara sugar

3 oz butter or margarine
3 oz black treacle
3 oz golden syrup
¼ pint milk
1 small egg

Grease and line a 7-in. square or round cake tin. Sift together the flour, salt, ginger and baking powder. Warm the sugar, butter, treacle and syrup until the butter melts, but do not overheat. Gradually stir this mixture into the dry ingredients, with the milk and beaten egg. Beat well. Pour into the tin and bake at 350°F (mark 4) for about 1 hour until well risen and firm to the touch. Cool on a wire rack.

Crunch-top cake

For the topping

2 oz plain flour
4 oz caster sugar

2 oz butter or margarine
4 level tsps cinnamon

For the base

12 oz plain flour
8 oz caster sugar
4 level tsps baking powder
a pinch of salt

6 oz butter or margarine
rind of 1 lemon, grated
2 eggs
6-fl. oz milk

Grease and line an 8-in. square cake tin. For the topping, sift the flour into a bowl and add the sugar. Rub in the fat, stir in the cinnamon and set aside.

To make the base, sift the flour, sugar, baking powder and salt together. Rub in the fat until the mixture resembles fine breadcrumbs, then add the lemon rind. Beat the eggs and milk together and pour on to the dry ingredients, mixing to a soft consistency. Turn the base mixture into the prepared tin and sprinkle with the topping. Smooth with the back of a spoon. Bake below the centre of the oven at 375°F (mark 5) for about 1 hour. If the cake shows signs of over-browning, cover with foil. Turn out carefully on to a cake rack lined with a clean tea towel. This cake should be eaten fresh.

Good Housekeeping's favourite Christmas cake

8 oz plain flour
½ level tsp ground cinnamon
½ level tsp ground mace
8 oz butter
8 oz soft brown sugar (dark or light)
rind of 1 lemon, grated
4 large eggs, beaten

8 oz currants
8 oz stoned raisins, chopped
8 oz sultanas
4 oz small glacé cherries, halved
4 oz mixed chopped peel
2 oz almonds, blanched and finely chopped
1–2 tbsps brandy

Grease and double-line an 8-in. round cake tin. Tie a band of brown paper firmly round outside and place on a baking sheet lined with brown paper, or place tin in another slightly larger tin and omit the brown paper. Sift together the flour and spices. Beat the butter until creamy, add the sugar and cream the mixture until fluffy. Add lemon rind and gradually beat in eggs. Fold in the flour alternately with the fruit and nuts. Finally stir in the brandy.

Turn the mixture into the prepared tin, and hollow the centre slightly. Bake below the oven centre at 300°F (mark 1–2) for about 3¾ hours. Allow to cool in the tin for 10 minutes, then turn out on to a wire rack to cool. To store, wrap in greaseproof paper and kitchen foil; a further 2 tbsps of brandy may be poured over the cake before storing.

Chocolate dot cake

6 oz butter
6 oz margarine
12 oz caster sugar
6 large eggs
few drops vanilla essence

8 oz self-raising flour
8 oz plain flour
2 tablespoons milk
6 oz chocolate dots

Grease and line a 9-in. square cake tin. Cream the fats and sugar, beat in the eggs one at a time, and add the vanilla essence. Sift in the flours and beat them in lightly with the milk. Fold in the chocolate dots. Turn into the prepared tin, level the surface and bake in the centre of the oven at 350°F (mark 4) for about 1 hour 20 minutes. After this time, cover the cake with double greaseproof paper or foil to prevent over-browning, and cook for a further $\frac{1}{2}$ hour. Turn out and cool on a wire rack.

Cherry slab cake

1 lb glacé cherries
6 oz butter
6 oz margarine
12 oz caster sugar

6 eggs
8 oz plain flour
8 oz self-raising flour

Grease and line a 9-in. square cake tin. Wash the cherries, dry thoroughly and halve. Cream the fats and sugar and beat in the eggs one at a time. Toss and coat cherry halves in about 2 tbsps of flour. Lightly beat the sifted flours into the creamed mixture, and place $\frac{1}{3}$ evenly in the base of the tin. Fold the cherries into the remaining $\frac{2}{3}$ and spread lightly over the plain mixture. Bake in the centre of the oven at 350°F (mark 4) for about 2 hours. If necessary, cover with a double thickness of greaseproof paper to prevent excessive browning.

Yacht birthday cake

Either of the two preceding recipes—*Chocolate dot cake* or *Cherry slab cake*—can be used to make this child's birthday cake. Cut the cake diagonally, then cut a small triangle from one half, $4\frac{1}{2}$ in. from the corner, leaving a narrow strip for the 'hull'. Make an apricot glaze from $\frac{1}{2}$ lb apricot jam and 2 tbsps water heated gently together and stirred until the jam softens. Sieve the mixture and bring it to the boil; continue to boil gently until glaze is of a suitable coating consistency. Cover each piece of the cake with the glaze and $1\frac{1}{2}$ lb ready-made almond paste, before finally coating with fondant icing (see below) or glacé icing. Keep back a little of the almond paste for the stripes and eyelets on the sails. The portholes are peppermint sweets.

Fondant icing

2 lb caster sugar
$\frac{1}{2}$ pint water

2 oz powdered glucose

Dissolve the sugar in the water over a low heat without boiling. Keep the sides of the pan free from sugar by 'washing down' with a wet pastry brush. Add the powdered glucose to the dissolved sugar and boil to 240°F without stirring. Cool slightly, then pour on to a wetted marble slab or other suitable heat-resistant surface.

When a skin begins to form round the edges, work the sides of the mixture up towards the centre, using a small spatula. Continue, collecting the syrup into as small a compass as possible, until it becomes white and malleable. Then knead it in the hands until it has a silky sheen. (If not required for immediate use, the icing can be kept in a plastic-lidded container.)

To prepare it for coating, place the fondant in a bowl over a saucepan of hot water, but don't let it get hotter than 98°F. Add enough—about 2 oz— sugar syrup (made by dissolving 2 oz caster sugar in $\frac{1}{8}$ pint water) to give a coating consistency. Colour about one-third of the fondant blue and use this to coat the hull. Coat the sails with uncoloured fondant. The sea is made from a little 'roughed-up' royal icing. Royal icing is also used for the name and 'Happy Birthday', and for sticking on the eyelets and portholes.

(See picture on page 104.)

SMALL CAKES AND COOKIES

A variety of little iced cakes looks attractive set out on a plate and certainly small children love them. However, they do tend to be rather 'fiddly' to make. If you need to produce a batch for a birthday party or other special occasion you can adapt the recipe for *Victoria sponge sandwich* (see previous cake section) and cook it as a slab; you can then ice it, decorate it and slice it into various shapes.

Victoria sponge slab

Double the quantities given for *Victoria sponge sandwich* and bake the mixture in a tin measuring 9-in. by $13\frac{7}{8}$-in. on the top at 350°F (mark 4) for 35–40 minutes.

Variations

Chocolate Slab: Add 1 oz cocoa, blended with a little water to a smooth paste, to the creamed mixture.

Pink Slab: Make up the recipe as given, but add a few drops of cochineal.

If wrapped in kitchen foil, these slab cakes will keep moist for several days, until you are ready to finish them.

Making small cakes from a slab

Chocolate Triangles: Cover the top of the cake with chocolate butter cream, made with 3 oz butter, 6 oz icing sugar and 1–1½ oz melted chocolate. Mark it with a fork and decorate with halved blanched almonds. Trim the edges, cut the cake in 2-in. strips and cut the strips into triangles.

107

Coffee Diagonals: Coat the top of the cake with coffee glacé icing. When this is nearly set use stiff coffee icing (using half the usual amount of water) to pipe double lines 1½ in. apart across the cake. In between, sprinkle grated chocolate or chocolate vermicelli. Trim the cake with a knife dipped in hot water, then cut into 1½-in. strips. Cut the strips across diagonally.

Lemon Squares: Cover the top of the cake with lemon butter cream, made with 3 oz butter, 6 oz icing sugar and a little lemon rind and juice. Decorate with chopped pistachio nuts or crystallised lemon slices. Trim the edges of the cake and cut into 1½-in. strips; cut the strips into squares.

Quick Petits Fours: Cut the cake into 2-in. strips and decorate the sides and top of each strip, finally cutting the strip into various shapes, with some decoration on each piece. (It is easier to cut the iced cake neatly if you use a knife dipped in hot water.) The sides of the cake can be spread with butter cream or jam and covered with chopped nuts or coconut. Here are a few ideas:

1 Put a long roll of almond paste along the top of the strip, fix it in place with jam and coat the strip with glacé icing.

2 Cover the top with butter cream, glacé icing or whipped sweetened cream and decorate with glacé cherries, angelica, nuts or small sweets; repeat the decoration down the strip.

3 Sandwich two small strips of contrasting-coloured cake together with jam or butter cream before decorating—for instance, chocolate and lemon, or raspberry and vanilla.

Cup cakes

4 oz self-raising flour
4 oz butter or margarine
4 oz caster sugar

2 eggs, beaten
nuts, fruit, to taste
(see variations below)

Place 12–16 paper cases in patty tins—this keeps them in good shape—or on baking trays. Cream the fat and sugar until pale and fluffy and add the egg, a little at a time, beating well after each addition. Fold in the flour and nuts, fruit or other flavours. If necessary, add a little milk to give a dropping consistency. Fill the cases ⅔ up and bake towards the top of the oven at 375°F (mark 5) for 15–20 minutes until golden.

Variations

Add 2 oz of one of the following: sultanas; chopped dates; chopped glacé cherries; chocolate chips; or chopped or crystallised ginger.

Lemon Cherry Buns: Add 1 level tsp grated lemon rind with the sugar. After baking, decorate with lemon-flavoured glacé icing and a piece of glacé cherry.

Orange Buns: Add 1 level tsp grated orange rind and decorate after baking with orange glacé icing.

Coconut Buns: Replace 1 oz of the flour with desiccated coconut. Decorate after baking with glacé icing and sprinkle generously with desiccated coconut.

Chocolate Buns: Replace ½ oz of the flour with cocoa and decorate with chocolate glacé icing.

Butterfly Cakes: Make the basic recipe and when cool, cut a slice from the top of each and pipe a butter icing rosette in the centre. Cut each cake slice in half and replace at an angle to represent wings. Dust with icing sugar.

Orange top hats

3 oz butter or margarine
3 oz caster sugar
1 large egg
1 level tsp grated orange rind

5 oz self-raising flour
1 tbsp orange juice
butter cream (2 oz butter, 4 oz icing sugar)

(Makes about 12)

Grease 12 2½-in. patty pans. Cream the butter and sugar, beat in the egg and orange rind. Lightly beat in the flour alternately with the orange juice. Half-fill the patty pans and bake just about the oven centre at 400°F (mark 6) for 15–20 minutes. Turn out and cool on a wire rack. When cold, use a small cutter to remove a 'hat' from each cake. Pipe a whirl of butter cream into the centre, dust lightly with icing sugar, and place the 'hat' back in position on top.

Butterscotch brownies

2 oz blended white vegetable fat
7 oz light, soft brown sugar
1 egg, beaten
3½ oz plain flour
1 level tsp baking powder

½ level tsp salt
¼–½ tsp vanilla essence
1½ oz shelled walnuts, coarsely chopped

(Makes about 24)

Grease and line a cake tin measuring 8-in. square by ½-in. deep. Melt the fat over a low heat. Remove from the heat and blend in sugar. Allow to cool, then stir in the egg. Sift together the flour, baking powder and salt and stir into the ingredients in the pan. Mix in the vanilla essence and the walnuts. Turn into the prepared tin and bake in the oven at 350°F (mark 4) for about 20 minutes. Cool in the tin before cutting into squares.

Coconut cherry mouthfuls

8 oz plain flour
1 level tsp baking powder
4 oz glacé cherries, quartered
1½ oz desiccated coconut
4 oz butter or margarine

3 oz caster sugar
¼–½ tsp vanilla essence
1 large egg, beaten
2 tbsps milk
desiccated coconut and cherries,
  for decoration

(Makes about 3 dozen)

Sift together the flour and baking powder. Stir in the cherries and coconut. Cream the butter and sugar, beat in the vanilla essence and egg and blend in a quarter of the dry ingredients. Finally fold in the remaining dry ingredients and milk. Drop tsps of the mixture in some more coconut to coat them and top with a quartered cherry. Bake on greased baking sheets at 375°F (mark 5) for about 15 minutes.

Coffee whirls

6 oz butter
2 oz icing sugar, sifted

2 level tsps instant coffee granules
6 oz plain flour

(Makes about 12)

Cream the butter and sugar until soft and light, then beat in the coffee granules. Gradually work in the flour. Put the mixture into a forcing bag fitted with a small vegetable star nozzle. Pipe little whirls on greased baking sheets, leaving a small hole in the centre of each. Leave in the refrigerator for at least 1 hour, then bake in the oven at 325°F (mark 3) for about 25 minutes. Cool on a wire rack. Serve plain, dusted with icing sugar, or sandwich in pairs with melted chocolate.

Walnut crunchies

3 oz butter
5 oz Demerara sugar
1 large egg

1 tbsp coffee essence
3 oz walnuts, finely chopped
6 oz self-raising flour

(Makes about 36)

Cream the butter and beat in the Demerara sugar until thoroughly blended. Then beat in the egg. Stir in the coffee essence, walnuts and flour. When well blended form into a roll 9-in. long, working on a lightly floured surface. Wrap the roll in foil or greaseproof paper and chill in the refrigerator until required; it should be cooked within 3 days.

To cook, remove from the refrigerator, slice thinly, place well apart on greased baking sheets and bake at 400°F (mark 6) for about 10 minutes.

Date crunchies

8 oz stoned dates, chopped
1 level tbsp honey
4 tbsps water
1 tbsp lemon juice
a pinch of powdered cinnamon

6 oz self-raising flour
6 oz fine semolina
6 oz butter or margarine
3 oz caster sugar

(Makes about 8)

Cook the dates, honey, water, lemon juice and cinnamon together until the dates are soft. Mix the flour and semolina. Warm the butter and sugar together in a small pan and stir it into the flour and semolina. Press half this mixture into a greased shallow 7-in. tin, cover with the date mixture and then top with the remainder of the flour mixture. Press down lightly. Bake at 400°F (mark 6) for about 35 minutes. Cut into rectangles and remove from the tin when cold.

(See picture on page 112.)

Grantham gingerbreads

4 oz butter or margarine
12 oz caster sugar
1 large egg, beaten

9 oz self-raising flour
1 level tsp ground ginger

(Makes about 30)

Cream the butter, add the sugar and beat until soft and well blended. Beat in the egg. Stir in the flour and ginger, sifted together, and work with the hand to a firm, but pliable, dough. Roll into balls the size of a walnut. Place on greased baking trays, keeping them apart to allow for spreading. Bake towards the top of the oven at 300°F (mark 2) for about 40 minutes until lightly browned and puffed up; these biscuits have a hollow centre. Cool on a wire rack.

(See picture on page 112.)

Meringues

2 egg whites
2 oz granulated sugar

2 oz caster sugar

(Makes about 12–16 meringue shells)

If preferred, use caster sugar only for your meringues—i.e., 4 oz. Line a baking tray with kitchen foil or with silicone (non-stick) paper. Whisk the egg whites very stiffly, add the granulated sugar and whisk again until the

Left: Date crunchies. Right: Grantham gingerbreads *(see page 111)*

mixture regains its former stiffness. Fold in the caster sugar very lightly, using a metal spoon. Pipe through a forcing bag—or put in spoonfuls—on to the baking sheet and dry off in the oven at 250°F (mark $\frac{1}{4}$) for several hours.

The meringues should be firm and crisp but still white. If they begin to brown, prop the oven door open a little. After about 2 hours' baking lay the meringues on their sides to dry out underneath. When ready, remove from the oven and cool on a wire rack.

Variations
1 Tint pink by adding 1–2 drops of red colouring with the sugar.
2 Make coffee meringues by adding 1 tsp coffee essence to each egg white, when the sugar is folded in.
3 For chocolate meringues, add cocoa with the caster sugar; allow 1 level tsp per egg white.

Using up the Yolks: The yolks left over from making meringues can be used up in omelettes, scrambled eggs, milk pudding, rissole mixtures, pastry, mashed potato and biscuits. If you have a fair number to use up try making lemon curd—much better than the bought version.

QUANTITIES FOR BASIC RECIPES
Scones
$\frac{1}{2}$ lb plain flour, and 3 level tsps
baking powder
or:
$\frac{1}{2}$ lb self-raising flour and 1 level
tsp baking powder

or:
$\frac{1}{2}$ lb plain flour
and 1 level tsp cream of tartar
and $\frac{1}{2}$ level tsp bicarbonate of soda

Use one of the above combinations of flour and raising agents with $\frac{1}{2}$ level tsp salt, $1\frac{1}{2}$–2 oz margarine or butter and $\frac{1}{4}$ pint milk.

Batter for pancakes

4 oz flour
1 egg

$\frac{1}{2}$ pint milk, or milk and water
$\frac{1}{4}$ level tsp salt

Coating batter

4 oz flour
1 egg

$\frac{1}{4}$ pint milk
a pinch of salt

Rubbed-in cakes

$\frac{1}{2}$ lb self-raising flour
$\frac{1}{2}$ level tsp salt
3–4 oz butter or margarine

3 oz sugar
1 egg
$\frac{1}{4}$ pint milk (roughly)

Coffee marble cake *(see page 103)*

Victoria sandwich

4 oz self-raising flour
4 oz butter or margarine

4 oz caster sugar
2 large eggs

Shortcrust pastry

½ lb plain flour
a pinch of salt
2 oz margarine

2 oz white fat
4 tbsps water (roughly)

Note: when a recipe says '8 oz shortcrust pastry' it means 8 oz flour plus the fat, etc.

Suetcrust pastry

½ lb self-raising flour
½ level tsp salt

4 oz shredded suet
8 tbsps cold water (roughly)

Crumble topping

¼ lb plain or self-raising flour
2 oz butter or margarine

1–2 oz sugar

Rich shortcrust pastry

½ lb plain flour
a pinch of salt
6 oz butter or margarine and lard

2 level tsps caster sugar
2 eggs

Crumb crust

8 oz digestive biscuits, or
   gingernuts, or cornflakes

3 oz butter, melted
2 oz sugar

Meringues

For meringue topping: Allow 1–1½ oz caster sugar to each egg white.
For shells: Allow 1 oz caster sugar and 1 oz granulated sugar to each egg white (or use all caster sugar, doubling the quantity).

Milk puddings

1½ oz rice, tapioca, sago or semolina to 1 pint milk.

Custards

Pouring: 2–3 eggs   1 oz sugar
          1 pint milk
Baked: 2–3 eggs, or 2 whole eggs   1 pint milk
             and 1 yolk   1 oz sugar

Sauces

Pouring: 1 oz flour   1 pint milk
          1 oz butter
Coating: 2 oz flour   1 pint liquid
          2 oz butter
Binding (panada): 4 oz flour   1 pint liquid
                4 oz butter

6 BREAKFASTS AND SUPPERS

This chapter gives some suggestions for the children's first and last meal of the day, but it could equally well be called 'Meals round the Clock'. A child will happily munch a peanut butter sandwich at any hour of the day, and bacon tastes just as good to him at supper as at breakfast-time. And with different members of the family coming and going at odd hours, there is a particular need for ideas for the 'flexible' snack. You will find some recipes for these adaptable dishes at the end of this chapter.

So although some of the following suggestions have been grouped under breakfast or supper, many of them would do equally well at other times of the day. Our old friend, the sandwich, is the most adaptable snack of all, and a number of ways of preparing it and filling it are included.

BREAKFAST

SWISS APPLE MUESLI: Overnight, soak 4 level tbsps rolled oats in $\frac{1}{4}$ pint natural fruit juice or water. Next morning, grate 2 eating apples, leaving the peel on, and mix with the oats. Add 4 tbsps top of the milk, 1 tbsp honey, a little brown sugar and 2 oz sultanas or raisins. Put into 4 glasses and sprinkle with chopped nuts.

INDIVIDUAL EGGS AND BACON: Partly grill the bacon rashers and put them in ramekins or a patty pan. Break an egg into each and bake in a moderate oven for 10 minutes. Serve turned out on to buttered toast.

ACCOMPANIMENTS FOR BACON: Bananas cut lengthwise can be fried in bacon fat. Crisply fried croûtons make a change from fried bread.

BREAKFAST PUFFS: Mix seasoned self-raising flour with enough water to make a dropping consistency, and fry spoonfuls in the hot bacon fat. Add a little onion or celery salt for extra flavour.

FISH AND BACON ROLLS: Flake some cooked smoked haddock and use it to stuff rolls of bacon; secure the rolls with cocktail sticks and grill.

FISH STEAK WITH GRAPEFRUIT: Grill and top with strips of crisp bacon and grapefruit sections.

FISH AND CHEESE: Poached smoked cod or haddock can be topped with a thin slice of red Cheshire cheese.

FISH AND SCRAMBLED EGG: Top waffles or toast with scrambled egg and flaked cooked fish; sprinkle with paprika.

KIPPER TOAST: Toast one side of the bread and put fresh or thawed kipper fillets on the untoasted side, covering the bread completely. Spread with a little butter and grill for a few minutes. Top with tomato slices and grill just long enough to cook the tomato.

PANCAKES: Serve small pancakes with grilled bacon and eggs, or with mushrooms and scrambled eggs or with kidneys and tomatoes. Slightly larger pancakes can be spread with butter and topped with sliced banana sprinkled with brown sugar, or with golden syrup or marmalade.

MEAT ROLLS: On days when there isn't time to make a cooked breakfast, serve oven-crisped rolls with a filling of cold ham, liver sausage or cheese.

SUPPER

BAKED EGGS AND MUSHROOMS: Sauté some sliced mushrooms in a little butter, spread them in a shallow ovenproof dish, season and break some eggs over them. Bake until set.

EGGS IN BATTER: Cut hard-boiled eggs in half lengthwise, brush the cut side with beaten egg and fix a thin slice of ham or tongue cut to the shape of the egg. Dip in coating batter and fry in deep fat.

STUFFED HARD-BOILED EGGS: Remove the yolks, mix them with a few drops of anchovy essence, or mashed sardines, or liver sausage, and replace them. Serve on buttered toast.

SARDINE TOASTS: Spread the toast with sardines mixed with a little cooked spaghetti, tomato sauce and Cheddar cheese, plus a squeeze of lemon and a dash of seasoning.

FISH BALLS: Flake cooked fish (fresh or smoked) and mix with an equal quantity of boiled rice. Season well and bind with beaten egg. Form into balls and shallow-fry.

SAVOURY FISHCAKES: Mix some cooked white fish with an equal quantity of white breadcrumbs. Season, add chopped parsley and some finely chopped cooked mushrooms. Bind with beaten egg, coat with egg and breadcrumbs, and fry until golden brown. Smoked fish is good in fishcakes, too.

KIPPERS IN BATTER: Cut some kipper fillets in neat pieces and dip in frying batter. Fry until crisp and brown. Sardines can be treated in the same way.

KEBABS: This is a good way to use up savoury odds and ends. Allow a skewer for each person and thread a selection of the following ingredients on to each skewer: bacon rolls, small sausages, tomatoes, mushrooms, cubes of luncheon meat and small onions. Include something sweet such as pineapple cubes. Brush with oil and grill under moderate heat for 10–12 minutes.

STUFFED DINNER ROLLS: Cut a piece off the top of each roll and scoop out the inside. Brush inside and out with butter or margarine, and crisp in the oven. Fill with a mixture of fish or meat bound with sauce (or condensed soup).

Tea-Time for Tots

A young child's tea may be his last meal of the day, so he needs some savoury snack along with the sweet things. Here are a few ideas:

TOAST FINGERS, spread with a little butter, yeast extract and grated cheese.

MINIATURE HOT DOGS, using half chipolatas with bridge rolls.

FRIED INITIALS: Make bread and cheese more interesting by cutting each child's initials from half-inch-thick slices of bread. Dip these in melted butter or margarine, and toss them in grated cheese. Bake on a greased baking sheet at 400°F (mark 6), for about 15 minutes, until crisp and golden.

Toasted sandwiches

Toast a thick slice of bread on both sides. Split it open with a knife and butter the untoasted sides. Spread a filling over one half, top with the other, and cut into fingers or squares.

FILLINGS: Scrambled egg and cooked ham; grilled bacon and mushrooms; sliced cooked sausage and tomato; sliced ham and chutney, etc.

OPEN TOASTED SANDWICH: Top with diced meat and cooked vegetables in white sauce, or chopped, cooked (or canned) meat which has been fried with slices of apple and sultanas, with a little curry powder.

WELSH RAREBIT: The basic topping mixture is 8 oz of Cheddar cheese, 1 oz butter, 1 level teaspoon dry mustard, salt and pepper, and 3–4 tablespoons brown ale. (If substituting milk for the ale, add a dash of Worcestershire sauce.)

Variations are Buck rarebit, which has poached egg on top, and Yorkshire rarebit, which has a slice of boiled bacon (or ham) between the cheese topping and the egg.

Sausage cabin *(see page 118)*

Fried sandwiches

FILLINGS: Fill, before frying, with minced ham and mustard, or bacon and chopped kidney, or with scrambled eggs and anchovies. With a chopped frankfurter filling, top with pineapple slices before serving.

FRENCH TOAST: Can be savoury or sweet. Dip slices of bread into a mixture of milk and beaten eggs (2 tablespoons to each egg) and fry until golden brown on both sides. Serve plain with grilled or fried bacon, sausages, tomatoes or kidneys, or top it with tomato sauce, or spicy fruit sauce. For the sweet version, sprinkle with cinnamon sugar, or spread with jam and cut into fingers.

ANY-TIME SNACKS

Sardine scrunchies

a can of sardines in olive oil
8-oz can spaghetti with tomato
cheese sauce
4 oz strong Cheddar cheese, grated
freshly ground pepper

1 small lemon
4 large thick slices white bread (from
a ready-sliced loaf)
parsley sprigs, for garnish

Drain the sardines, turn them into a bowl and break up with a fork. Add the contents from the can of spaghetti together with half the cheese. Season with freshly ground pepper; add a squeeze of lemon. Toast one slice of the bread. Turn the slices over and spread them with the topping, dividing it equally between them. Sprinkle the remaining grated cheese on top and grill under a medium heat, until golden. Garnish with lemon slices and parsley.

Sausage cabin

1 lb beef chipolatas
1 small onion, skinned and thinly
sliced
1 oz butter
2 oz cheese, grated

$1\frac{1}{2}$ lb potatoes, peeled
seasoning
1 egg, beaten
4 firm tomatoes
$\frac{1}{2}$ lb peas, cooked

Place the sausages in a baking tin and bake in the centre of the oven at 375°F (mark 5) until they are all well browned—about 25 minutes. Drain on kitchen paper. Melt half the butter in a small pan and fry the onion gently until soft, stirring occasionally. Cook and mash the potatoes, add the remaining butter and season well. Stir in the cooked onion, cheese and egg. Put a square of foil about the size of a serving plate on a baking sheet, turn the potato on to it and mould into a cabin shape. Flatten the sides with a palette knife. Cut the cooked sausages in half and press them into the sides of the potato cabin. Leave a little space for the door and save one sausage for a chimney.

118

Slice the tomatoes thinly and arrange them on the cabin 'roof' to look like tiles. Place the chimney at one end. Heat in the oven for 10 minutes, then lift the foil on to a plate. Garnish with freshly cooked peas.

This is a good dish to serve for a small child's birthday tea or supper. (See picture on page 117.)

Sausage sizzlers

8 large slices white bread
½ lb sausagemeat
2 tsps Worcestershire sauce
1 level tbsp tomato-chilli chutney

tomato slices
thinly sliced onion rings
parsley sprigs

Use ready-sliced bread for this recipe. Blend together the sausagemeat, Worcestershire sauce and chutney. Toast one side of each slice of bread; spread some of the sausagemeat right up to the edge of the untoasted side. Cook under the grill at medium heat, for about 5 minutes. Cut each sizzler in half and top with sliced tomato, onion rings and parsley sprigs.

Stuffed eggs Mornay

6 eggs
1 oz butter
2 tsps oil
2 tbsps chopped onion
4 oz mushrooms, chopped

2 level tsps tomato paste
2 tsps chopped parsley
seasoning
¾ pint cheese sauce
a little grated cheese

(Serves 4–6)

Hard-boil the eggs just before they are required; they should be hot. Heat the butter and oil and fry the onion until soft but not coloured. Add the mushrooms and cook until soft. Mix in the tomato paste, parsley and seasoning to taste. Cut the eggs in half lengthways and remove the yolks. Pound them into the mushroom mixture and use this to stuff the whites. Arrange in a dish, coat with the cheese sauce, dust with the grated cheese and brown under a hot grill. Serve with jacket potatoes and whole tomatoes.

(See picture on page 120.)

Potato scones

1 lb boiled potatoes
4 oz plain flour

salt to taste

Mash the potatoes, add the salt and knead in the flour. Roll out thinly on a floured board, cut into rounds and place on a greased baking sheet. Bake at

500°F (mark 9) for 10 minutes, turning halfway through. Serve hot with butter. Delicious with jam, honey, syrup, peanut butter, or cream cheese.

Nutty cheese teabread

8-oz carton cottage cheese, sieved
6 oz soft dark brown sugar
5 oz plain flour
3 level tsps baking powder
3 eggs, beaten

grated rind 1 orange
4 oz walnut halves
3 oz ground almonds
1–2 tbsps golden syrup

Grease a loaf tin measuring 9-in. by 5-in. at the top, and line it with greaseproof paper. Cream together the cheese and sugar. Sift together the flour and the baking powder and add alternately with the eggs. Stir in the orange rind and half the walnuts, chopped, and ground almonds. Turn into the prepared tin, level the surface and top with the remainder of the halved walnuts. Cook at 350°F (mark 4) for 1 hour 20 minutes. Cool for 10 minutes before removing from tin. Strip off the paper immediately. Brush with golden syrup while still warm. Cool on a wire rack.

Stuffed eggs Mornay *(see page 119)*

Malt fruit bread *(see below)*

Malt fruit bread

12 oz plain flour
$\frac{1}{2}$ level tsp bicarbonate of soda
1 level tsp baking powder
2 level tbsps Demerara sugar
4 level tbsps golden syrup

4 level tbsps malt extract
$\frac{1}{4}$ pint milk
9 oz sultanas, seedless raisins or
   chopped dates
2 eggs

Grease a loaf tin measuring 9-in. by 5-in. at the top. Sift together the flour, bicarbonate of soda and baking powder and add the sugar. Warm together the syrup, malt and milk; stir well blended, then allow to cool. Add the fruit to the flour, together with syrup mixture and eggs, beating until evenly mixed. Turn into the prepared tin and bake in the centre of the oven at 300°F (mark 2) for about 1$\frac{1}{2}$ hours. Turn out and cool on a wire rack. Store, wrapped in kitchen foil, for several days before serving sliced and buttered.

(See picture on page 121.)

7 MEALS FROM THE STORE CUPBOARD

Say you are just preparing supper for the two of you one evening when friends drop in on their way home from holiday. There are five of them, they are obviously hungry, and you have two cod steaks. Clearly, in this case two into five won't go.

There is only one way of coping with such situations—to plan for them before they arise. A well-stocked freezer, containing home-made dishes as well as commercially frozen ones is invaluable at such times—or indeed, when you need an instant meal for your own family. If you are fortunate enough to have one you will find some recipes at the end of this chapter for suitable dishes to store against unexpected arrivals.

The emergency shelf

But in any case, there is no need to be caught out provided you have an emergency shelf in your store cupboard. It is a good plan to keep some ingredients for instant meals separately from the rest of your stores, and to make a point of replacing them as soon as they are used. If you jot down a few menus and pin your notes inside the cupboard, it will forestall the slightly panicked feeling which underlines your welcoming smile on such occasions.

The point of an emergency shelf is to supplement your ordinary standbys, such as eggs, cheese, rice and pasta. Since a meal made out of, say, corned beef and instant potato needs a 'lift' to disguise its origins, your shelf should include a wide variety of herbs, flavouring and seasonings. Some useful items to stock are listed in the table opposite.

Although it is perfectly possible to produce a pleasant meal entirely from your store cupboard, it will be better balanced if you can offset a course made from cans and packets with a salad or fresh fruit.

Some ideas for the savoury course

CANNED MINCED BEEF can be used to make spaghetti Bolognese, with canned tomatoes, or for shepherd's pie.

122

Cans for hors d'oeuvre

Pâté
Artichoke hearts
Anchovy fillets

Cans for the main course

Chicken
Ham
Stewed beef
Minced beef
Corned beef
Steak pie filling
Pork luncheon meat
Pork sausages
Frankfurters
Meat balls
Tuna
Salmon
Sardines
Crabmeat
Herrings

Cans for accompaniments

Tomatoes
Sweetcorn
Asparagus tips
Celery hearts
Pimento
Carrots
Potatoes
Green beans
Mushrooms

Cans and packets for sauces:

Consommé
Condensed vegetable
  soups
Tomato juice
Instant potato
Bolognese sauce
Curry sauce
Apple sauce
Roux mix

For seasoning and flavouring

Dried sliced onions
Dried celery flakes
Dried peppers
Dried mushrooms
Dried basil, chives,
  tarragon, thyme
Garlic powder
Curry powder
Paprika
Celery salt
Anchovy paste
Tomato paste
Soy sauce
Sage and onion
  stuffing
Worcestershire sauce
Chutney
Beef and chicken stock
  cubes
Pickled onions
Parmesan

Cans, jars and packets for dessert

Fruit
Pie-fillings
Evaporated milk
Condensed milk
Milk puddings

Cake mixes
Shortbread mix
Instant desserts
Macaroons
Ratafia biscuits

For flavouring and decorating

Plain chocolate
Angelica
Crystallised cherries
Marshmallows
Sherry or Kirsch

CANNED PORK SAUSAGES, with baked beans and canned tomatoes, can be put in a casserole and topped with cheese scones, then baked in the oven. A pinch of dried basil improves the flavour of the tomatoes.

CANNED CHICKEN can be made into a fricassee, with a rich white sauce and canned or frozen vegetables.

CANNED SALMON OR TUNA can be mixed with cooked macaroni, cheese sauce and a little lemon juice; make a breadcrumb topping and put under a hot grill to heat through and crisp.

PANCAKES are good filled with crisp bacon, onion, tomato and Worcestershire sauce blended together. Alternatively, fill them with creamed corn, cheese and olives, or sardines with a little chopped onion and pimento.

UNSWEETENED SCONE MIX, with herbs and grated cheese, can be used to make a light pizza. Or it can be mixed with suet instead of butter to make miniature dumplings.

SAGE AND ONION STUFFING, from a packet, can be used in place of coating crumbs for rissoles.

INSTANT POTATO can be piped to make a quick finish to a main dish, or for making into Duchesse potatoes. It is also handy as a basis for cream soups—such as watercress, or Vichyssoise, and for thickening other soups quickly.

CANNED CONDENSED SOUPS, made up to half-strength, make quick sauces.

ROUX MIX is a useful shortcut to making white sauce.

Canned, frozen and dehydrated vegetables

CANNED POTATOES are often improved by being sautéed or deep-fried; or simply heat them through with a little butter and a squeeze of lemon juice.

PEAS: Cook, and serve with chopped, skinned tomatoes and spring onions lightly fried in butter. Or cook some chopped celery in $1\frac{1}{2}$ in. of water until tender, add a packet of peas and cook for a further 5 minutes.

PEAS AND CARROTS: Lightly fry a chopped onion in butter and add to the cooked vegetables.

CUT GREEN BEANS: Slice 2 oz mushrooms and fry in butter. Cook the beans, then add the mushrooms.

SLICED GREEN BEANS: Add some crisply fried bacon and chopped cooked onion to the cooked beans.

SWEET CORN KERNELS: Mix the cooked corn with 2 tbsps double cream.

Ideas for quick desserts

CAKE MIXES can be used for steamed and baked sponge pudding. A shortbread mix makes a good base for a fruit-topped dessert or a rich flan case; it can also be used as a crumble topping.

CANNED MILK PUDDINGS can be made more interesting if flavoured with fruity jams. Creamed rice is improved by folding in a can of fruit salad, drained, and chilling.

CANNED PINEAPPLE PIECES can be used to make fritters. Drain and add them to a crisp batter mixture; fry spoonfuls and then toss the fritters in sugar and cinnamon.

INSTANT DESSERT MIXES can be combined with canned, stewed or fresh fruit, or fruit filling. Make up a packet and fill individual glasses with alternate layers of fruit and dessert.

APPLE PIE-FILLING: Mix the apple with sultanas and a pinch of mixed spice and use it to fill a double-crust pie. Glaze the crust with milk and sprinkle with brown sugar.

CANNED PEACH HALVES: Drain and sauté the halves in butter until golden, then pile ice cream on top. Add some sherry to the fruit syrup and use it as a sauce.

BUTTERSCOTCH SAUCE to serve with ice cream can be made by heating together 2 oz of soft brown sugar and $\frac{1}{2}$ oz of butter until they bubble, and then adding a small can of evaporated milk. Cook gently, stirring, until the sauce becomes creamy.

MARSHMALLOW AND APPLE SAUCE: Heat a can of apple sauce, then stir in some marshmallows, cut in pieces. Top with ice cream, or whipped cream, and sprinkle with nutmeg or cinnamon.

EVAPORATED MILK can be whipped to produce a creamy topping, if first chilled.

THE SAVOURY COURSE
Individual beef cobblers

15-oz can stewed steak
salt and pepper
10-oz can tomato juice
8 oz flour
1 level tsp baking powder

1 level tsp mixed herbs
2 oz fat
a little milk, or milk and water
a little beaten egg, to glaze

Put a rounded tbsp of steak into each of 4 individual casseroles and add some well-seasoned tomato juice. Bake at 425°F (mark 7) for 15 minutes. Meanwhile, add seasoning and the herbs to the flour and baking powder. Rub in the fat and add enough liquid to form a soft dough. Knead lightly and cut into rounds. When the meat is bubbling well, remove from the oven and arrange the savoury scones on top. Brush with beaten egg and bake for a further 7–10 minutes.

Puff-topped steak pie *(see page 126)*

Puff-topped steak pie

8-oz packet frozen peas
15-oz can stewed steak and gravy
   pie-filling
1 level tbsp flour

2 tbsps water
garlic salt, if liked
2 level tsps dried onion flakes
7¾-oz can whole carrots, drained

For the topping

½ pint water
½ oz butter
2½-oz packet instant potato

2 eggs, separated
salt and pepper

Cook the peas according to the directions on the packet, and drain. Empty the can of meat into a 7-in. pie-dish and spoon the gravy into a small pan; if the gravy is thick, heat the contents gently until it can be drained off. Blend the flour and water to a smooth paste, stir in the gravy and return it to the pan. Bring to the boil, stirring, and season with garlic salt. Add the onion flakes. Roughly chop the carrot and combine with the gravy, then fold into the meat. Spoon the peas over the meat.

To make the topping, boil the water and add butter and instant potato. Remove from the heat and beat to absorb the water, then whip in egg yolks and season. Whisk the egg whites until stiff and fold them into the potato, using a metal spoon; it should be light and fluffy. Top the pie with the potato mixture, forming this into peaks. Bake at 450°F (mark 8) for about 15 minutes until golden. Serve with lightly cooked cabbage dabbed with soured cream.

(See picture on page 125.)

Corned beef flan

1 8-oz packet shortcrust pastry mix
1 packet cheese sauce mix
½ pint milk

12-oz can corned beef, diced
5-oz can garden peas, drained

Make the pastry as directed and use to line a 7-in. flan ring or sandwich tin. Bake blind at 425°F (mark 7) for 15 minutes. Meanwhile, prepare the sauce mix using the milk. Arrange the corned beef and peas in the partly baked flan case and coat with the sauce. Replace in the oven for a further 15 minutes. Serve in wedges.

Herring hotpot

1 lb potatoes, peeled
2 7-oz cans herrings in tomato
   sauce

8-oz can tomatoes
7-oz can sweetcorn kernels, drained
a little melted butter

Parboil the potatoes, then slice them thinly. Put the herrings, tomatoes and sweetcorn in layers in a shallow ovenproof dish. Cover with overlapping slices of potato, brushed with melted butter. Place under a moderate grill until golden-brown and heated through—about 20 minutes.

Tuna pizza

6-oz packet scone mix
7-oz can tuna, drained
2 level tbsps tomato paste
6½-oz can mushrooms, drained
   and dried

3½ oz Cheddar cheese, grated
1¾-oz can anchovies
chopped parsley

(Serves 4–6)

Line the base of a deep 8-in. sponge cake tin with 2 strips of foil about 2½ in. wide, forming a cross in the base (the pizza can then be lifted out of the tin for serving). Make up the scone mix following the instructions on the packet and lightly press into the cake tin base. Blend the tuna with the tomato paste and spoon over the scone mixture. Add the mushrooms. Sprinkle with the cheese and arrange the anchovies on top. Bake at 450°F (mark 8) for about 20 minutes. Garnish with parsley.

Spanish omelette

1 small onion, skinned and finely
   chopped
a little olive oil
1 tomato, skinned and chopped
2 cooked potatoes, diced

2 canned pimentos, chopped
2 tbsps cooked peas
4 eggs
salt and pepper

(Serves 2)

Fry the onion lightly in a little oil. Add all the vegetables and cook for a few minutes, stirring. Whisk the eggs, season well and pour over the vegetables in the pan. Cook slowly, shaking the pan occasionally. When one side is lightly and evenly browned, turn the omelette over and cook the other side. Don't fold; serve hot, accompanied by a green salad.

If you find it difficult to turn the omelette, try this method. When the first side is browned, cover the omelette with a plate and turn the pan, omelette and plate over together, so that the omelette falls on to the plate. Turn the pan the right way up and slide the omelette off the plate back into the pan, browned side uppermost. Cook until the underside is golden; alternatively, the second side can be browned under the grill quite satisfactorily, if you find this easier.

Ham and cheese crempogs

(Welsh pancakes)

4 oz plain flour
a pinch of salt
1 egg
½ pint milk, or milk and water

a little lard
4 slices lean cooked ham
6–8 oz grated cheese
dried mixed herbs

Sieve the flour and salt into a bowl and make a well in the centre. Drop in the egg and add half the liquid by degrees, mixing to a smooth paste with a wooden spoon and gradually drawing in the flour from the sides. Beat the batter thoroughly for 5–10 minutes, then stir in the rest of the liquid.

Heat a little lard in a frying-pan until it is smoking hot. Pour in sufficient batter to cover the pan thinly and cook quickly until the pancake is golden-brown underneath. Turn it over and on the cooked side place a slice of ham and 1½–2 oz of the cheese, mixed with a pinch of dried herbs. Cook the second side, roll up the pancake and keep it hot while you make the rest of the pancakes. Serve at once with grilled tomatoes.

Left: Supper macaroni. Right: Butterscotch fruit sauce *(see opposite)*

Supper macaroni

1 medium-sized onion, skinned and
  chopped
1 oz lard
4 oz quick-cooking macaroni
salt
1 oz flour

½ pint stock made from a cube
8-oz minced beef
2 level tbsps tomato paste
3 oz Cheddar cheese, grated
sliced tomato, to garnish

Lightly fry the onion in the lard until soft. Meanwhile, cook the macaroni in boiling, salted water for 7 minutes. Add the flour to the onion and cook over a low heat for 2–3 minutes, stirring continuously. Gradually add the stock; bring to the boil, stirring until thick. Add the meat and tomato paste and heat through. Add the drained macaroni and half the cheese. Turn into an ovenproof pre-heated dish; garnish with a few slices of tomato and sprinkle with the remaining cheese. Grill until golden.

(See picture opposite.)

PUDDINGS AND DESSERTS

Lemon sundae

¼ pint double cream
small can sweetened condensed milk
6 tbsps lemon juice

grated rind of 1 lemon
a few brandy snaps

Lightly whip the cream, then stir in the condensed milk, lemon juice and rind. Divide between four glasses and chill. Decorate with roughly crushed brandy snaps.

Butterscotch fruit sauce (for ice cream)

8-oz can red cherries
8-oz can pineapple pieces
1 level tbsp cornflour

2 oz butter
6 level tbsps dark soft
  brown sugar

(Serves 3, using an 11-fl. oz block of dairy ice cream.)

Drain the cherries. If practicable, discard the stones, using a cherry-stoner. Drain the pineapple and reserve the juice. Blend the cornflour with the pineapple juice and put this in a small pan with the butter and sugar. Heat gently until butter has melted, then bring to the boil, stirring. Add the fruit and cook, while continuing to stir, for 2–3 minutes. For other ideas for sauces to serve with ice cream, see pages 99–101; many of these are made from ingredients from the store cupboard.

(See picture opposite.)

Fruit crunch

4 oz butter
4 oz Demerara sugar
6 oz rolled oats

14-oz can blackcurrant or apricot
   pie-filling
cream, or ice cream

Cream the butter, then stir in the sugar and oats. Place half the mixture in a greased 8-in. by 8-in. shallow tin and bake at 425°F (mark 7) for 10 minutes. Cover with the pie-filling, top with the remaining mixture and bake for a further 20 minutes. Serve warm, cut in squares and topped with cream.

Pineapple delight

6–8 macaroon biscuits, crushed
12-oz can crushed pineapple, drained
¼ pint cream or evaporated milk

½ pint of cold, thick custard
a few ratafia biscuits, to decorate

Put the crushed macaroons into 4 individual glasses, and place a rounded tbsp of crushed pineapple over them. Whisk the cream or evaporated milk, add to the cold custard and whip thoroughly. Fold in the remaining pineapple. Pile this mixture on to the macaroons; serve with ratafia biscuits.

Negritas

4 oz plain chocolate
3 eggs, separated
3 tbsps sherry or 1 tbsp brandy

a little whipped cream or grated
   chocolate, to decorate

Grate the chocolate and place in a bowl over a pan of hot water. Beat in the egg yolks and stir for several minutes, then remove from the heat and stir in the sherry or brandy. Whisk the egg whites until stiff and fold into the mixture. Pour immediately into glasses and leave to become cold. Serve decorated with cream or grated chocolate.

STAND-BYS FROM THE FREEZER

Meat balls in tomato sauce

1 lb fresh minced beef
¼ lb onions, skinned and finely
   chopped
½ clove garlic, crushed*

½ level tsp mixed dried herbs
salt and freshly ground black pepper
2 level tbsps plain flour
2 tbsps oil

For the tomato sauce

2 level tbsps cornflour
1 bay leaf

¾ pint beef stock
8-oz can tomatoes

In a large bowl combine the beef, onions, garlic, herbs and seasoning. Shape the mixture into about 26 small balls. Toss them in flour and fry them in oil until sealed and browned. Drain the meat balls. To make the sauce, stir the cornflour and any excess flour into the pan juices. Add the bay leaf, stock and tomatoes. Bring slowly to the boil, and sieve over the meat balls.

To freeze
Cool and spoon into a rigid container, then seal.

To re-heat
Turn the dish into a saucepan and heat gently, stirring occasionally, until just on the point of boiling—about 20 minutes.

Just before serving, blend in a 5-fl. oz carton of soured cream and re-heat without boiling. Creamed potatoes make a suitable accompaniment.

* If intending to store longer than 2 weeks, omit the garlic; it can be added to the sauce at the time of re-heating.

Stuffed pancakes

½ pint batter

lard for frying

For the filling

4 oz onion, skinned and finely
   chopped
½ oz butter
1 lb minced beef
1 large carrot, grated
2 level tbsps cornflour

14-fl. oz can tomato juice
salt and freshly milled pepper
½ level tsp each dried fines herbes
   and thyme
1 tsp soy sauce

Make 8 pancakes (about 7-in. in diameter) in the usual way (see *Puddings and Cakes* chapter), using ½ pint batter and a little lard. For the filling, sauté the onion in butter without browning, add the mince and cook until sealed, then add the carrot and cook for 5 minutes. Blend the cornflour with tomato juice and stir it in, then add the seasoning, herbs and soy sauce. Bring to the boil, reduce the heat and simmer, covered, for 10 minutes. Let the filling become cold, then use it to fill the pancakes and roll them up.

To freeze
Arrange the pancakes side by side in a baking dish; wrap them in a polythene bag or wrap over the dish with foil.

To serve
Sprinkle 1 oz grated réd Leicester cheese over the frozen stuffed pancakes. Cover with a lattice of thinly cut strips of canned red pimento and scatter another 1 oz of grated cheese over the top. Cover with a foil lid and cook in the oven at 375°F (mark 5) for about 15 minutes. Discard the foil and continue to cook until the pancakes bubble and the cheese is browned. Serve hot.

Berry mousse

a 1-pint raspberry jelly tablet
$\frac{1}{4}$ pint water

7$\frac{3}{4}$-oz can strawberries
6-fl. oz can evaporated milk

(Serves 4–6)

Place the separated jelly tablet in a bowl, add $\frac{1}{4}$ pint boiling water, and stir to dissolve. Sieve the berries and juice and add them to the jelly. When the jelly is about to set, fold in the evaporated milk, whisked until thick and creamy. When evenly blended, pour into a rectangular rigid polythene container.

To freeze
Cover with the lid, seal and label.

To serve
Turn it out and either serve it semi-frozen, decorated with piped whipped cream, or leave it to thaw in the refrigerator for 2 hours before decorating.

Egg custards

4 oz shortcrust pastry (4 oz flour, etc.)
$\frac{3}{4}$ pint milk

3 eggs
2 level tbsps caster sugar

(Serves 5)

Roll out and line 5 shallow foil pielet pans (4-in. size) with the pastry. Place on a flat tray. Whisk together the milk, eggs and sugar, strain into a jug and pour into the pastry shells.

To freeze
Place in the freezer on a tray until frozen, then wrap singly or stack in groups, using heavy duty plastic bags, before replacing in the freezer.

To cook
The custards can be cooked straight from the freezer. Add a pinch of grated nutmeg and cook at 325°F (mark 3) for 1–1$\frac{1}{4}$ hours. Serve warm or cold.

8 MEALS WITHOUT MOTHER

Sooner or later, father may have to be 'mother'—and if the children are still small, this change of role will involve a good deal more than presiding over the teapot. Mother may have been told that she must rest in bed, or be admitted to hospital suddenly, or simply be called away unexpectedly, leaving father to manage.

Although quite a few men nowadays pride themselves on being able to turn out one or two dinner-party dishes, this is not quite the same as coping

Father sometimes has to take over in times of crisis

with everyday family cookery; as they will soon find if they try to serve steak au poivre or Bombay curry to a three-year-old.

So this chapter is intended for the novice cook (whether father or an older brother or sister), who has to take over in an emergency. Unlike the general run of cookery instructions, which are likely to be difficult for a completely inexperienced person to follow, it assumes little or no previous knowledge.

Once the cooker has been mastered and a few basic techniques grasped, some useful ideas for quickly prepared meals will be found in *Breakfasts and Suppers* and *Meals from the Store cupboard*.

Tips on Temperature

At least 15 minutes before using the oven, light or switch on the oven at the temperature you're going to need. The correct heat throughout cooking time is vital. For top-of-the-stove cookery, avoid too fierce a heat, a common fault of the inexperienced cook. Water boils away, vegetables disintegrate, and pancakes and sausages burn all too easily if you try to cook them too quickly. You will also make work for yourself if you allow soups and other liquids to boil over and become encrusted on the cooker or let a saucepan get badly burned.

Timing

To serve a complete meal when the family want it and not just when you're ready to serve it isn't as difficult as it might seem. Keep to two courses, one of which will need no cooking. If you are serving roast beef, follow it with canned fruit or cheese biscuits, or fresh fruit. Alternatively, if you prefer to serve a cooked pudding, start the meal with cold meat and salad, or sausages and mashed potatoes, courses which you can prepare after putting the pudding into the oven.

Ice cream is a good stand-by for puddings; the vanilla kind can be topped with sweet sauces, jam, bramble jelly, chocolate vermicelli and chopped nuts, or served with a pie-filling.

Utensils and Equipment

If you have special utensils for non-stick pans, use them; and even if the makers claim that ordinary metal spoons and spatulas will not harm the non-stick surface, use them very carefully and don't scrape or scratch. Non-stick pans must not be cleaned with steel wool, metal scouring pads or scouring powders.

Wash up and put away utensils, so far as is possible, as you go along; in this way you will have more room in the kitchen for juggling with plates and dishes when it comes to dishing-up time. Get the non-cooks in the family to help here, by laying the table and clearing away afterwards. Washing up is best done as soon as possible. There are few things more calculated to spoil your enthusiasm for getting the next meal than having to face a kitchen cluttered with dirty crockery and cutlery.

Using convenience foods

A packet which claims to contain three servings may not satisfy you and two other members of the family. So it is a good idea to have something on hand with which to eke out the contents if necessary—extra canned meat or vegetables for a savoury course; canned fruit or ice cream for a dessert.

Always follow the instructions on the container regarding cooking and serving. Most things can be turned out of the cans and heated either in a saucepan or a double pan. (The latter, good for heating bottled or canned sauce for spaghetti, milk puddings, custards and so on, is equally good for melting chocolate cream bars for a quick sauce for ice cream.) If you haven't a double pan, tip the sauce, pudding or chocolate into a small pottery bowl which will sit firmly on and in the pan, allowing space for the water simmering gently below.

Take special care when opening square cans with the 'key' provided; or you may end up with a half-opened can which resists all attempts at opening with an ordinary can opener. If corned beef, luncheon meat, etc. is chilled in the refrigerator before serving it is much easier to slice.

Some basic cooking terms

BASTING: Moistening meat or poultry during roasting by spooning over it the juices and melted fat from the tin; the purpose is to prevent the food from drying out, to add extra flavour and to improve the appearance.

BLENDING: Mixing flour or cornflour to a smooth cream with a cold liquid—milk, water or stock—before adding a boiling liquid. This is done to prevent lumps forming when preparing soups, stews, gravy, and some sauces.

BOILING: Cooking in liquid—usually stock, water or milk—at a temperature of 212°F. Vegetables, pasta and rice require boiling.

BROWNING: Giving a dish, usually already cooked, an appetising golden-brown colour by placing it under the grill or in a hot oven for a short time.

PARBOILING: This means that the food is boiled for part of the normal cooking time, the cooking then being completed in another way.

REDUCING: Stock and other liquids are sometimes required to be 'reduced' in volume, in order to concentrate the flavour and make the basis of a sauce. This is done by simmering the liquid so that some evaporates.

SHREDDING: Foods such as cheese or raw vegetables often need to be sliced into very fine pieces; a sharp knife or coarse grater is usually used.

SIMMERING: To keep a liquid just below boiling point—at about 205°F or 96°C. The liquid is first brought to the boil, then the heat adjusted so that the surface of the liquid is kept just moving or 'shivering'.

STEWING: A long, slow method of cooking in a liquid which is kept at simmering point; particularly suitable for coarse-fibred foods. The liquid is served with the food, so none of the flavour is wasted. Stewing is carried out in a good strong pan or a casserole with a tightly-fitted lid. The food should not be boiled, as this causes it to break up or to become tough.

STOCK: The liquor in which meat, bones or vegetables have been simmered to extract the goodness and flavour. Ready-prepared cubes provide a con-

Cod kebabs *(see page 140)*

venient substitute and may be used in most recipes which call for stock. Use a chicken or beef cube, whichever is more suitable for the particular dish. Remember that stock cubes contain salt, so any seasoning you may add must be adjusted accordingly; taste before you add the seasoning specified in the recipe.

THICKENING: Giving body to soups, sauces or gravies by the addition of flour, cornflour or arrowroot; these must first be blended.

MEAT

How to roast a joint
You need to check the weight in order to calculate the cooking time. Put the joint in a roasting tin, arranged so that the largest cut surfaces are exposed and the thickest layer of fat is on top. This helps to baste the joint automatically. If the meat is lean, spread a little dripping over the surface. Arrange the oven shelves so that the joint goes in the centre of the oven. Don't prick the meat with a fork or other sharp utensil while it is cooking, or you'll lose some of the juices. (Use two spoons if you want to turn or lift the joint.)

Beef
High Temperature Method (suitable for sirloin, ribs, rump and topside): For meat on a bone, cook at 425°F (mark 7), allowing 15 minutes per lb plus 15 minutes over if you want the meat to be lightly done. Allow 20 minutes per lb, plus 20 minutes for medium-done meat. If the joint has been boned and rolled, allow 25 minutes per lb, plus 25 minutes over.

Moderate Temperature Method (for the same cuts): For meat on the

136

bone, cook at 375°F (mark 5) for 25 minutes per lb for medium to well-done result. If the joint has been boned and rolled, allow 30 minutes per lb.

Slow Roasting Method (for cheaper cuts such as brisket and flank): For cuts on the bone, allow 40 minutes per lb at 325°F (mark 3) to give a medium to well done result. If the joint is boned and rolled, allow 45 minutes per lb.

Lamb

Suitable cuts for roasting are leg, shoulder, and loin. Heat the oven to 350°F (mark 4) and allow 27 minutes to the lb and 27 minutes over for meat on the bone. If the joint has been boned and rolled, allow 35 minutes to the lb and 35 minutes over. Lamb is served well-done.

Chicken

If frozen, allow it to thaw completely. Don't forget to remove the packet of giblets tucked away inside. Sprinkle the cavity with a little salt and put a knob of margarine or butter inside, with a thick wedge of lemon, or an onion. Brush the skin with melted butter, margarine or salad oil, and season with salt and pepper.

Place on a rack in a shallow roasting tin. Roast at 375°F (mark 5), allowing 20 minutes per lb, plus 20 minutes over. Test the chicken for tenderness by piercing the thickest part of the thigh with a skewer. If the juices are almost colourless, the bird is ready; if they're tinged pink, more cooking is needed.

Roasting in Foil: This keeps the meat moist and tender, but the foil should be opened during the last half hour of cooking time so that the joint can become crisp and brown. Follow the instructions on the roll.

Roasting in Bags (or Film): Another way of ensuring moist meat with, this time, a crisper outside. Follow the directions on the packet, which should include instructions to sprinkle flour in the bag or on the film; this prevents the bag bursting.

How to make gravy

Most children love gravy and will probably make a fuss if you serve almost any kind of meat without it. If you are very short of time, they will be quite happy if you use a gravy mix. However, the proper way to make it when roasting a joint is from the residue in the roasting tin.

After removing the joint pour off the surplus fat, and put the tin on one of the rings on top of the stove. Add ½ pint of stock or vegetable water, and stir over a low heat to mix well. If you want a thick gravy, blend 2 level tsps of flour or cornflour with the stock or water (add the liquid to the flour a little at a time), before adding it to the juices. Then cook, while stirring, for a few minutes until it thickens.

If using foil or roasting film, scrape the residue and juices into a saucepan and follow the above instructions.

Sausages

They don't have to split. Separate them carefully, and don't prick them. Melt $\frac{1}{2}$ oz lard or cooking fat in a frying-pan and fry the sausages very gently over a low heat. Allow about 20 minutes for thick ones, 12 for thin; the skinless type take about 10 minutes. Don't be tempted to prod them, but turn them occasionally to ensure they are cooked through and evenly browned.

Sausages can also be grilled. Pre-heat the grill pan, and grill them on the rack under a medium heat, allowing the same cooking time as for frying. Turn them frequently. If you want to cook a large number of sausages, you can bake them in a greased baking tin, in the centre of the oven, at 400°F (mark 6), for about $\frac{1}{2}$ hour.

VEGETABLES

Open a can or packet, if you feel harassed. Canned vegetables should be heated in a pan just long enough to be heated through evenly, and drained. Baked beans need stirring in order to prevent sticking and burning. When cooking frozen vegetables, follow the instructions on the packet exactly. Don't overcook vegetables, whether fresh, frozen or canned; ideally they should be served as soon as cooked, but if you have to keep them hot they can be placed in a metal colander over a saucepan of hot water; put a lid over the colander. Here are the basic methods of cooking potatoes; for other fresh vegetables see appropriate chapter.

Potatoes

Peel them as thinly as possible, with a peeler or a sharp, short-bladed knife. Scrape or brush new potatoes. Cook them as soon as possible after preparing them; if they have to stand for a while, keep them under water to prevent discoloration. Allow 6–8 oz per portion.

Boiled: Cut into even-sized pieces, put into just enough cold water to cover them and add $\frac{1}{2}$ level teaspoon of salt per lb. Bring to the boil and simmer the potatoes until they are tender but not broken: 15–20 minutes for new potatoes, 20–30 minutes for old. Test by piercing with a thin cooking fork; if it slides in easily, the potatoes are ready. Drain well, and add a knob of butter before serving.

Mashed: Boil old potatoes as directed above; drain and dry over a low heat, then mash with a fork or potato masher.

Creamed: Mash with a knob of butter or margarine, salt and pepper to taste, and a little milk. Beat well over a gentle heat with a wooden spoon until fluffy.

Baked: This is as easy a way as any, provided you remember to get them into the oven early enough. For method, see *Baked stuffed potatoes* in *Vegetables* chapter.

Roasted with the Joint: Use old potatoes. Peel and cut them into even-sized pieces and parboil them by cooking in salted water for 5 minutes. Drain the potatoes well and put them into the roasting tin with the meat, about 40 minutes before the meat is due to be ready.

Basic beef casserole

$1\frac{1}{2}$ lb chuck or blade steak
1 oz flour
salt and pepper
1 tsp mustard

1 oz dripping
1 pint stock
2 onions, skinned and sliced

Cut the steak into pieces of a convenient size for serving and roll them in seasoned flour. Melt the dripping in a pan and brown the meat. Place in an ovenproof dish. Add any remaining seasoned flour to the residue in the pan and cook for 1–2 minutes. Gradually add the stock, stirring. Pour over the meat and add the onions. Cover and cook at 350°F (mark 4) for $1\frac{1}{2}$–2 hours.

Variations
1   Simmer the stock to reduce it by half and add a 14-oz can of tomatoes.
2   Use half stock and half any left-over beer or red wine, plus $\frac{1}{4}$ to $\frac{1}{2}$ lb button mushrooms. (Toddlers may not like this flavour.)
3   Add a topping of creamed potatoes or dumplings.

French-style roast chicken

$2\frac{1}{2}$–3 lb roasting chicken
3 oz butter or margarine
salt and pepper
5–6 sprigs parsley or tarragon

3 oz butter or margarine, melted
2 rashers of bacon
$\frac{1}{2}$ pint chicken stock, made from a
   stock cube

Prepare the bird as for ordinary roasting. Cream 3 oz butter or margarine with a good sprinkling of salt and pepper and put the butter and sprigs of herb inside the bird. Brush the breast with melted butter and cover with the rashers of bacon. Place the bird in a roasting tin and add the stock. Bake in the centre of the oven, basting with the stock every 15 minutes. Remove the bacon during the last 15 minutes of the cooking to brown the breast. Retain the stock to make gravy.

   The bird can be cooked in a roasting bag, which saves basting.

Red-hots

3 tbsps cooking oil or 2 oz lard
1 lb Frankfurters
8 tbsps tomato ketchup

2 level tbsps made mustard
long soft bread rolls (allow 1 for each
   Frankfurter)

Heat the oil or fat in a heavy frying-pan and fry the Frankfurters until browned. Mix the ketchup with the mustard and spoon this over them. Turn the Frankfurters so that the sauce coats them and heat for 2–3 minutes. Serve in long soft rolls which have been split, buttered and toasted.

Cod kebabs

1 packet cod balls in batter
small can mushrooms
4 rashers streaky bacon
4-in. skewers

8 cocktail sticks
15-oz can baked beans
a knob of butter
chives

Thread 3 cod balls on each skewer, with a mushroom in between each one. Cut the rind off the bacon and stretch each rasher by running the back of a knife along it on a flat surface. Wrap the bacon around each filled kebab skewer and fix the ends with cocktail sticks to keep it secure. Pre-heat the grill until it is really hot. Grill the kebabs on the rack for about 10 minutes, turning them round once or twice to make sure they are evenly cooked.

Open the can of beans and heat them in a non-stick pan; stir gently until they are really warm. Add the butter and then pour the beans into four warm, shallow bowls. Put a cooked kebab on top of each one, carefully removing the skewer just before serving. Garnish with spikes of chives. Fish fingers, cut in halves, can be used in place of cod balls in this recipe.

(See picture on page 136.)

Tomato-cheese omelette *(see page 143)*

Beefburger decker

1 bloomer loaf
3 packets of 4 frozen beefburgers
1 tbsp oil
$\frac{1}{2}$ lb onions, skinned and sliced
6 oz Lancashire cheese, grated

1 level tsp cornflour
2 tbsps milk
$\frac{1}{2}$ lb tomatoes, cut in
   thin slices
4 anchovy fillets

Cut 8 slices from the loaf, cutting at an angle across the slashes on top in order to give elongated slices. Fry the beefburgers in the oil in a large frying-pan for about 10 minutes, turning them halfway through cooking time. Remove them from the pan and keep them warm. Add the onions to the pan and fry until soft and just beginning to colour.

Meanwhile, blend the grated cheese, cornflour and milk together. Toast the bread until golden. Spread the cheese mixture over half the slices, grill until the cheese starts to melt, top with slices of tomato, and return the slices to the grill until golden. Butter the remaining slices of toast and top each with 3 beefburgers and the onions. Place the lids on top and garnish with curled anchovies.

(See picture below.)

Beefburger decker *(see above)*

Scrambled eggs on toast

1 oz butter
4 eggs

4 tbsps milk
salt and pepper

(Serves 2)

Melt the butter in a small thick pan over a low heat. Put the eggs, milk, salt and pepper into a bowl and whisk them, then pour into the pan. Stir slowly, keeping the heat gentle until the mixture just begins to thicken. Meanwhile make the toast and keep it hot. Remove the eggs from the stove and stir until creamy. Butter the toast, pile the scrambled eggs on to it and serve at once.

Variations
All sorts of extra ingredients can be added to this basic dish, to provide variety. To the above mixture add 2 oz of one of the following: mushrooms, sliced and lightly fried; tomatoes, skinned, chopped and lightly fried with a diced rasher of bacon; ham, tongue, or other cooked meat, chopped; pork sausages, cooked and sliced; Finnan haddock (or other smoked fish) cooked, boned, skinned and flaked; shrimps, shelled; cheese, grated, or $\frac{1}{2}$ level tsp dried herbs, or 1 level tbsp finely chopped mixed fresh herbs.

Omelettes

Allow 2 eggs per person. Whisk the eggs lightly, season with salt and pepper and add 1 tbsp water. Heat the frying-pan* gently and when it is hot add a knob of butter to grease it lightly. Pour the beaten eggs into the hot fat. Stir gently with a fork, the back of the prongs held against the base of the pan so that the liquid egg can flow to the sides and cook. When the egg has set, stop stirring and cook the omelette for another minute until the underside is golden-brown.

It is at this stage that any filling is placed on top. With a palette knife, fold the omelette by flicking one-third over to the centre, then folding the opposite third to the centre. Turn the omelette on to a plate, folded side underneath. When making filled omelettes it may be easier simply to fold it in half.

Fillings and flavourings
FINES HERBES: Add 1 level tsp mixed dried herbs to the beaten egg mixture before cooking.

CHEESE: (1) Grate $1\frac{1}{2}$ oz cheese and mix 1 oz with the eggs before cooking; sprinkle the rest over the omelette after it is folded.

(2) Melt 2 oz grated cheese, 1–2 tbsps milk and $\frac{1}{2}$ oz butter over a low heat; add $\frac{1}{2}$ level tsp dry mustard or $\frac{1}{4}$ tsp vinegar before using as a filling.

TOMATO: Chop 2 tomatoes and fry them in butter for 4–5 minutes until

* Use a 6-in. pan for a 2-egg omelette, an 8-in. pan for 4–5 eggs and a 10-in. one for 8 eggs.

soft and pulped. Add salt, pepper, and a pinch of rosemary, sage or mixed herbs.

MUSHROOM: Wash and slice 2 oz mushrooms and cook in butter in a saucepan until soft. Place in the centre of the omelette before folding it over.

BACON: Rind and chop 2 rashers of bacon and fry in a saucepan until crisp. Use as above.

BACON AND APPLE: Lightly fry 2–3 diced bacon rashers with 1 diced apple until tender; add a dash of lemon juice.

SMOKED HADDOCK: Flake some cooked smoked haddock and heat gently in cheese sauce.

TUNA FISH: Flake a small can of tuna fish and mix with a little condensed mushroom soup.

KIDNEY: Skin, core and chop 1–2 sheep's kidneys, add 1 tsp finely chopped onion and fry lightly in a little butter in a saucepan until tender.

HAM OR TONGUE: Add 2 oz chopped meat and 1 tsp chopped parsley to the beaten egg before cooking.

TOMATO-CHEESE: Slice 2 tomatoes and place on the omelette. Sprinkle with finely grated cheese and place under the grill to melt the cheese.

(See picture on page 140.)

Corned beef salad

1 lettuce
2 eggs
a few spring onions
a few radishes

2 tomatoes
some cucumber
small can of corned beef,
    cubed

Remove the outside lettuce leaves. Wash the rest under a running tap, put into a salad basket and shake out as much water as possible. Set aside in a cool place until needed. Hard-boil the eggs by simmering them in a pan of water for 10 minutes. Plunge them into cold water and peel them immediately; cool in cold water and cut in slices. Trim the spring onions and cut off the stalks to about 3-in. in length. Remove the radish roots and cut the stalks to about $\frac{1}{2}$-in. in length; wash them and put them in a bowl of clean water. Slice the tomatoes and cucumber. Place a few lettuce leaves on each person's plate, then arrange portions of the other ingredients on the lettuce, piling the meat in the centre.

THE SWEET COURSE
Baked stuffed apples

4 cooking apples
2 oz sultanas

2 oz brown sugar
1$\frac{1}{2}$–2 oz margarine

Wipe the apples and make a shallow cut through the skin round the middle of each. Remove the cores and fill the holes with a mixture of sultanas, brown sugar and margarine. Wrap each in a little parcel of foil and stand the 'parcels' in an ovenproof dish or baking tin. Bake at 400°F (mark 6), until soft: from $\frac{3}{4}$–1 hour. (Children will probably want packet custard with this.)

Chocolate crackles

8 oz chocolate dots　　　　　　　**2 oz butter**
1 oz golden syrup　　　　　　　　**2 oz cornflakes**

Melt the chocolate dots with the syrup and butter in a pan, over a very low heat. Do not let the mixture boil. When smooth, fold in the cornflakes. Divide the mixture into 12 heaps, placing them on a greased plate or baking sheet, and leave until set.

Bread and butter pudding *(opposite)*

Bread and butter pudding

8 large slices of bread
1½ oz butter or margarine
2 oz currants
2 oz sultanas
1 pint milk
(Serves 4–6)

2 oz caster sugar
2 eggs
¼ tsp vanilla essence
grated nutmeg
Demerara sugar

Remove the crusts from the bread, and butter the slices. Cut each slice into four triangles. Arrange alternate layers of bread, buttered side uppermost, with the fruit in a 2½-pint ovenproof dish until it is half filled. Add the sugar to the milk and heat until it is dissolved. In a small basin, beat the eggs and vanilla essence together, add this to the warmed milk, blending together thoroughly. Strain this custard over the bread and sprinkle the top with grated nutmeg. Bake in the oven at 350°F (mark 4) for about 1¼ hours, until brown and set. Sprinkle the pudding with Demerara sugar and serve at once.

(See picture on page 144.)

Fruit crumble

1–1½ lb apples or plums
2–3 oz sugar, for the fruit
1–2 tbsps water

3 oz butter or margarine
6 oz plain flour
3 oz sugar, for the crumble

Peel and slice the apples, or chop and stone the plums. Arrange the fruit and sugar in layers in a greased 1½-pint ovenproof dish, and add the water. For the topping, rub the fat into the flour until the mixture forms fine breadcrumbs, then add the sugar. Sprinkle this mixture evenly over the fruit, pressing it down lightly. Bake in the centre of the oven at 375°F (mark 5) for 25–30 minutes.

Pinwheel trifles

1 small bought jam-filled Swiss roll
13½-oz can crushed pineapple

15-oz can custard

Cut the Swiss roll into 12 slices and press firmly into the base of four glasses. Drain the juice from the pineapple and spoon it over the Swiss roll so that it soaks in thoroughly. Divide the crushed pineapple between glasses. Top with a layer of custard.

9 SHOPPING AND STORING

When and where you chose to do the main, basic shopping will probably depend on the availability of the family car, unless you are lucky enough to have an obliging grocer who will still deliver. The convenience and 'fringe benefits' of the old fashioned corner shop—which may perhaps still deliver or even be willing to cash a cheque on a Saturday morning because you are personally known—may well outweigh the advantages of lower prices at your local supermarket. It doesn't always pay to shop around; if you are very busy it can actually be wasteful of time and energy.

If you try to reduce your weekend shopping to a minimum, and do as much as possible during the week, you will save money since prices tend to rise on Saturday. The middle of the week is a good time, too, to take a close look at seasonal fluctuations in prices of meat, fish, fruit and vegetables. If you suddenly find that there is a glut of tomatoes or sweetcorn, or perhaps that some luxury such as globe artichokes or avocados have fallen sharply in price, it is worth re-thinking your menus for the week to take advantage of them.

Some advice on choosing specific foods have been given in the appropriate preceding chapters, but here are a few general considerations to bear in mind when doing your shopping.

Quantities to allow per person for one meal

8–12 oz meat on bone
6–8 oz boneless lean meat
3–4 oz cooked sliced meat or sausage
3 oz mince, etc., for made-up dishes
8–12 oz chicken
4 oz liver
8 oz whole fish
4 oz fish fillets
6 oz root vegetables
6 oz runner beans

6–8 oz sprouts, cabbage or spring greens
12 oz peas in pod
14 oz fresh spinach
2 oz each of pasta, rice, lentils, dried peas and beans
4–5 oz fruit in pies, puddings or compôtes
$\frac{1}{4}$ pint milk in milk puddings, moulds or jellies

(Quantities of meat, fish and poultry should be doubled or trebled if planning for leftovers, as recommended in chapter 1.)

146

FOOD VALUES

Group	Sources	Why necessary
Proteins	Meat, poultry, fish, eggs, milk, cheese. Some vegetables (e.g. peas, beans, lentils) are fair sources.	Needed for body-building and 'repairs'; particularly important for children.
Fats and Oils	Butter, margarine, cheese, cream, full cream milk, cooking fats and oils, fat meat and oily fish.	These are a concentrated source of heat and energy; some also contain vitamins A and D.
Carbohydrates	Starchy foods: (flour, bread, cakes and biscuits, cereals, potatoes and pulses). Sugary foods: honey, jam and marmalade; golden syrup, treacle, confectionery, fruit.	These also provide heat and energy, and account for 50 60 per cent of our total calorie intake.
Minerals and trace elements		
Calcium	Milk, cheese and other milk products. Also eggs, green and root vegetables and fish.	Needed for formation of bones and teeth, and for general growth.
Iron	Liver, kidney, heart and other meat; eggs, wholegrain cereals. Fish, pulses, green vegetables and potatoes.	Needed to keep the blood in good health. Especially important in pregnancy.
Sodium and potassium	Main source of sodium is common salt; also found in cheeses, yeast and beef extracts, corned beef, ham. Nuts, dried fruits yield potassium.	Helps maintain correct balance of body fluids. Potassium also aids muscles and heart rhythm.

Group	Sources	Why necessary
Phosphorus	These essential substances are found in many of the foods which go to make up a good mixed diet.	Helps maintain bones, nails, teeth.
Iodine		Constituent of a substance in the thyroid gland.
Fluorine	Occurs naturally in some drinking water, especially in hard water areas.	Helps protect teeth against decay.
Magnesium	Green vegetables, lentils, whole grains.	For healthy teeth, bones; nervous stability.
Vitamins Vitamin A	Liver, butter, margarine, eggs, milk, cheese, carrots, spinach and many green vegetables, watercress, dried apricots and prunes, some fish liver oils.	Necessary for growth and development; for healthy functioning of the eyes and for keeping mucous membranes, skin, glands and bones healthy.
Vitamin B complex	Yeast and yeast extracts; wholegrain cereals and wheat grain preparations; offal, lean meat, egg yolk, milk, vegetables, nuts and fruit.	For keeping nervous system, digestion and other processes in good condition and for maintaining appetite.
Vitamin C	Blackcurrants, rosehip syrup, oranges and orange juice con-centrate, strawberries, tomatoes, lemon juice, gooseberries and other soft fruits. Sprouts, cauliflower, spinach and watercress.	Increases resistance to infection and keeps skin in healthy condition.

Group	Sources	Why necessary
Vitamin D	Main source is sun-light, the ultra-violet rays converting a substance present in the skin into this vitamin. Also in fish liver oils, oily fish, egg yolk, butter, margarine.	Needed for the utilisation of calcium and phosphorus, to ensure healthy teeth and bones.
Vitamin E	Wheat germ, whole grains, nuts.	Concerned with fertility: may affect ageing process.

Saving money

Is It Really An Economy? Buying packaged foods for family use doesn't necessarily mean going for the so-called economy sizes. If half the contents go stale before the packs are used up, they are a luxury. But family packs of cornflakes, instant coffee, cornflour—especially those 'own-name' brands offered by multiple stores and supermarket chains—do show a saving if they are family favourites.

Bulk Buying: Large quantities of food and household products can be bought at lower than normal retail prices through some mail order firms, 'cash and carry' stores and for the freezer owner, through specialist frozen food firms. If you can take advantage of these facilities, they may help you to economise. But don't let a tempting price blind you to such considerations as your housekeeping budget—can it stand such a heavy outlay at one time? —or the space you have available. You might find yourself tending to use foods extravagantly, simply because they are there. Or your family might take against a previously popular food, long before the supply is used up. According to a survey carried out recently by the Consumer Association, some shoppers have found that goods bought in this way actually cost them *more*, not less.

Probably the best way to benefit from bulk-buying is to combine with neighbours before placing an ambitious order. In this way you can take advantage of the low prices without being overwhelmed by the quantities— stowing away 72 toilet rolls, for instance, might take up more space than you bargained for.

Convenience Foods: If you need to work to a strict budget, you may feel that these are a sinful luxury, except in an emergency. This isn't always true; frozen fish, for instance, is often better value than it may seem from the size of the pack, since wastage is eliminated. And if you live some distance away from a fishmonger, it may be a great advantage to buy your fish along with your groceries. If a ready-made product such as puff pastry is a boon, why not take advantage of it? If you really can't make something of which there is a perfectly good commercial version, there is no point in wasting valuable time on it when you could be turning out the dishes at which you know you excel. Packet desserts are another great time-saver.

Eggs, the oldest convenience food of all, and richer in food value than many, are still the most useful for any time of day when a quick snack is needed. So make sure you keep a good store in your larder. Similarly, cheese needs little or no preparation, and is a very good source of protein.

Store cupboard sense
Planning for family meals also means planning the store cupboard—and the freezer, too, if you have one. Your store cupboard should complement the fresh foods in the larder and refrigerator, and should ensure, too, that emergencies can be faced with comparative equanimity. Keep a good, basic selection of cans, packaged foods and bottles. If you have a freezer make sure that you maintain stocks of the commercially frozen foods which you find most worthwhile for your family, plus, of course, a selection of home-made dishes, in family-size and individual servings.

Use your stores in rotation and examine them from time to time to check their condition and to see if they need replenishing. A note pad on the inside of the larder or cupboard door helps you to keep track.

How long will they keep?
Storage demands care to ensure that, whether fresh, packaged, cooked, canned or frozen, the foods will be in good condition when you eat them. Perishables need special care, of course, but it's also important to know how best to store the other foods.

A refrigerator, where the temperature discourages the growth of micro-organisms, is best for perishable foods, but as that temperature doesn't destroy micro-organisms which are already present in the food, everything that goes into it should be as fresh as possible—and should go into it as soon as possible after purchase. Storage times and methods vary, but this chart gives you an idea of how to deal with different foods.

REFRIGERATOR STORAGE TIMES

Food	How to store	Days
MEAT, RAW		
Joints	Rinse blood away; wipe dry,	3–5
Chops, cut meat	cover loosely with polythene or foil	2–4
Minced meat, offal	Cover as above	1–2
Sausages	Cover as above	3
Bacon	Wrap in foil or polythene, or put in plastic container	7

Food	How to store	Days
MEAT, COOKED		
Joints	In tightly wrapped foil or polythene,	3–5
Sliced ham	or in lidded container	2–3
Continental sausages	As above	3–5
Casseroles	In lidded container	2–3
POULTRY, RAW		
Whole or joints	Draw, wash, wipe dry. Wrap loosely in polythene or foil	2–3
POULTRY, COOKED		
Whole or joints	Remove stuffing; when cool, wrap or cover as for cooked meats	2–3
Made-up dishes	Cover when cool	1
FISH, RAW (white, oily, smoked)	Cover loosely in foil or polythene	1–2
FISH, COOKED	As above, or in covered container	2
SHELLFISH	Eat the day it is bought—don't store	
VEGETABLES, SALADS		
Prepared green and root vegetables, green beans, celery, courgettes, aubergines, peppers	In 'crisper' drawer, or in plastic container, or wrapped in polythene	5–8
Sweetcorn, mushrooms, tomatoes, radishes, spring onions	Clean or wipe as necessary; store in covered container	5–7
Lettuce, cucumber, cut onions, cut peppers, parsley	As above	4–6
Cress, watercress	As above	2
FRESH FRUIT		
Cut oranges, grapefruit, lemons	In covered container	3–4
Strawberries, redcurrants, raspberries, peaches	As above	1–3
Grapes, cherries, gooseberries, cut melon	As above	5–7
Rhubarb, cleaned	As above	6–10
EGGS		
Fresh, in shell	In rack, pointed end down	14
Yolks	In lidded plastic container	2–3

	Larder storage	
Whites	As above	3–4
Hardboiled, in shell	Uncovered	up to 7
FATS		
Butter, margarine	In original wrapper, in special compartment of refrigerator	14–21
Cooking fats	As above	28
MILK, ETC		
Milk	In original container, closed	3–4
Cream	As above	2–4
Soured cream, buttermilk, yogurt	As above	7
Milk sweets, custards	Lightly covered with foil or film	2
CHEESE		
Parmesan, in piece	In polythene film, foil, or airtight container	21–28
Hard cheeses	As above	7–14
Semi-hard cheeses	As above	7–10
Soft (cream or curd) cheeses	As above	5–7
BREAD, ROLLS, ETC.		
Any type of bread	In original waxed paper or polythene wrapper, or in foil	7
Sandwiches	Wrap in foil or use tightly lidded plastic box; do not store if filling contains mayonnaise	1–2
LEFTOVERS		
Casseroles, pies, vegetables, cooked fruit	In original dish, tightly covered, or in plastic container	2–4
Canned foods, opened	Leave in can but cover; fruits and fruit juices, which tend to alter slightly in flavour, are best put in another container	As for freshly cooked foods
STAND-BYS		
Batter, uncooked	In covered jug or plastic container	1–2
Pancakes, cooked	Interleaved with greaseproof paper and foil-wrapped	7
Dry pastry mix	In screwtop jar or plastic container	up to 14
Pastry, raw	Wrapped in foil	2–3
Grated cheese	In lidded jar or plastic container	up to 14
Stock, soup	In covered jug	1–2

Larder storage

For short-term housing of perishables, the temperature should not be higher than 10°C (50°F). Fish, meat, poultry, milk and cream should be stored in a larder for only about a day; cover them as for refrigerator storage.

Pet foods such as cereals and biscuits should not be kept in the larder; any infestation which might be present could spread to other commodities. If this happens, all affected foodstuffs must be destroyed and the container washed, sterilised and thoroughly dried before using again.

In the following chart, the 'keeping' times given for packets, jars or cans refer to the unopened container. Many canned foods remain sound for longer periods than those advised here, but if they are stored over-long the flavour and texture may suffer.

LARDER AND FOOD CUPBOARD STORAGE TIMES

Food	Keeping qualities, time	Storage comments
Flour, white	Up to 6 months	Once opened, transfer
Wheatmeal	Up to 3 months	to container with
Wholemeal	Up to 1 month	close-fitting lid
Baking powder, bicarbonate of soda, cream of tartar	2–3 months	Dry storage essential; if opened, put in container with close-fitting lid
Dried yeast	Up to 6 months	As above
Cornflour, custard powder	Good keeping qualities	As above
Pasta	As above	As above
Rice, all types	As above	As above
Sugar, loaf, caster, granulated	As above	Cool, dry storage; if opened, transfer as above
Sugar, icing, brown	Limited life—tends to absorb moisture	Buy in small quantities, as required
Tea	Limited life—loses flavour if stored long	Buy in small quantities; store in airtight container in dry, cool place
Instant and ground coffee in sealed can or jar	Up to 1 year	Cool, dry storage; once opened, re-seal securely; use quickly
Coffee beans, loose ground coffee	Very limited life; use immediately	Buy as required; use airtight container

Food	Keeping qualities, time	Storage comments
Instant low-fat skimmed milk	3 months	Cool, dry storage is vital; once opened, re-seal securely; use fairly quickly
Breakfast cereals	Limited life	Buy in small quantities. Cool, dry place
Dehydrated foods	Up to 1 year	Cool, dry place. If opened, fold packet down tightly and use within a week
Herbs, spices, seasonings	6 months	Cool, dry storage, in airtight container. Keep from light. Buy in small quantities
Nuts, ground almonds, desiccated coconut	Limited life—depends on freshness when bought. Fat content goes rancid if kept too long	Lidded container
Dried fruits	2–3 months	Cool, dry storage
Jams, etc.	Good keeping quality	Dry, cool, dark storage
Honey, clear or thick	As above	Dry, cool storage. After about 1 year, appearance may alter, but still eatable.
Golden syrup, treacle	As above	As above
Condensed milk	4–6 months	Safe even after some years, but caramellises and thickens. Once opened, harmless crust forms; cover can with foil lid and use within 1 month
Evaporated milk	6–8 months	Safe even after some years, but darkens, thickens and loses flavour. Once opened, treat as fresh milk
Canned fruit	12 months	Cool, dry place
Canned vegetables	2 years	Cool, dry place

Food	Keeping qualities, time	Storage comments
Canned fish in oil	Up to 5 years	Cool, dry place
Canned fish in tomato sauce	Up to 1 year	Cool, dry place
Canned meat	Up to 5 years	Cool, dry place
Canned ham	6 months	As above. Cans holding 2 lb or more should be kept in refrigerator
Pickles, sauces	Reasonably good keeping qualities	Cool, dry, dark place
Chutneys	Limited life	As above
Vinegars	Keeps at least up to 2 years	Cool, dry, dark place; strong light affects flavoured vinegar and produces a non-bacterial cloudiness. Re-seal after use; never return unused vinegar to bottle
Oils (olive, corn)	Up to 18 months	Cool, dry place

Home Freezer: As with other forms of storage, the length of time varies according to the particular food. Some foods can be stored for longer periods than others; after the optimum period there is still no risk to health, but flavour and quality will deteriorate. Freeze only the things which you know you will make full use of, and which will save time; turn a glut of tomatoes, for instance, into a Bolognese sauce, packing it in meal-size quantities if your family likes Spaghetti Bolognese. Store meat casseroles in family sizes or individual servings. It's also useful to store meat or chicken stocks—and sliced bread is handy in an emergency. All foods must be correctly packed, whether in polythene, foil, or plastic or waxed containers.

Here are some general points about packing:

1 Packs should be of a practical size, since once opened, they must be used up straightaway.

2 Allow ½ in. head space for expansion with liquids, and with any foods packed in liquid.

3 Exclude as much air as possible before sealing.

4 Label each pack carefully with contents and date.

5 Make an inventory of the contents of the freezer to ensure using foods in the correct order.

(For detailed guidance on home freezing, see Good Housekeeping *Home Freezer Cook Book.*)

HOME FREEZER STORAGE TIMES

Food		Time
VEGETABLES, FRUIT		Up to 1 year; use up before new season's supply arrives
MEAT, UNCOOKED	Beef	8 months
	Lamb	6 months
	Pork, Veal	6 months
	Mince	3 months
	Tripe, Offal	3 months
	Sausages, cured vacuum-packed bacon	3 months
	Vacuum-packed smoked bacon	1 month
MEAT, COOKED	Casseroles, Stews, Curries	2 months
POULTRY, UNCOOKED	Chicken	12 months
	Duck, Turkey	6 months
	Giblets	3 months
GAME (AFTER HANGING)		6 months
FISH (FREEZE WITHIN 24 HOURS OF CATCHING)	White fish	6 months
	Oily (Salmon, Trout, etc.)	4 months
DAIRY PRODUCE	Eggs without shell, separated	10 months
	Butter, unsalted	6 months
	Butter, salted	3 months
	Cream (40% butterfat and over)	12 months
	Soft cheese	8 months
	Hard cheese	3 months
PREPARED FOODS	Baked bread	1 month
	Baked cakes	6 months
	Baked pastry	6 months
	Uncooked pastry	3 months
	Soups, sauces, stocks	3 months
	Home-made	3 months
ICE CREAM	Commercially made	1 month

INDEX